50 THINGS TO DO WHEN YOU TURN 50

SELLERS

PUBLISHING

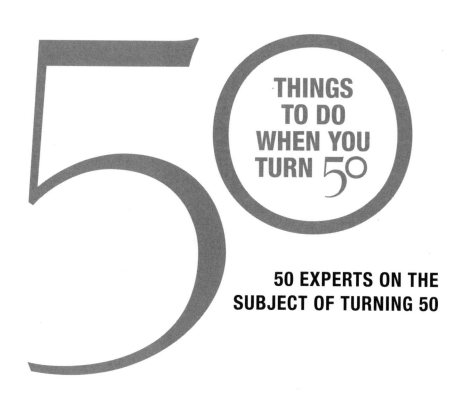

THINGS TO DO WHEN YOU TURN 50

50 EXPERTS ON THE SUBJECT OF TURNING 50

EDITED BY RONNIE SELLERS

Commissioning Editors
ALLISON KYLE LEOPOLD • GERIT QUEALY
DEBRA GORDON • BRIAN O'CONNELL

Series Editor
SARAH MAHONEY

Sellers Publishing, Inc.
161 John Roberts Road, South Portland, Maine 04106
For ordering information:
(800) 625-3386 toll-free
(207) 772-6814 fax

Visit our Web site: www.sellerspublishing.com
E-mail: rsp@rsvp.com

Robin Haywood: Publishing Director
Mary Baldwin: Managing Editor
Cover Design by: Sowins Design, California
Interior Design by: Faceout Studio, Oregon

The following essays are reprinted with permission of the publishers:
Find your inner elegy (pp. 31) was originally published as "Fiftieth Birthday Eve" from
The Art of Drowning by Billy Collins, © 1995 and is reprinted with permission from the
University of Pittsburgh Press. *Keep a sense of adventure* (p. 34) by Marianne Williamson
originally appeared in *The Gift of Change* © 2004 by Marianne Williamson and is
reprinted with permission of HarperCollins Publishers, Inc. *Take your self back* (p. 54)
was originally published in *Fear of Fifty* by Erica Jong, © 1994 and is reprinted with
permission of HarperCollins Publishers, Inc. Continued on page 303.

ISBN 13: 978-1-4162-0611-8
Library of Congress Control Number: 2010921821

Printed and bound in the United States of America.

Contents

SECTION FIVE   137
MANAGING YOUR CAREER AT MIDLIFE

Introduction

Remember when you subscribed to the "never trust anyone over 30" philosophy? Maybe you didn't live in a commune, as I did, go to weeklong music festivals or protest in the streets with thousands of other zealous Baby Boomers. But in your mind, you knew you were different than your parents. You belonged to a new generation, one that was unique, one that had its own destiny, one that simply could not be understood by anyone over 30.

By the time you actually turned 30, you were probably so immersed in your career and your family that you didn't have time to consider that you were now one of *them*. Besides, you hadn't lost your idealism, you merely redirected it into activities that were . . . well . . . more profitable.

You can still remember what you did on your 40th birthday, but the details are a little fuzzy. You certainly looked and felt better than your parents did when they were 40, and you were still a decade away from having to worry about being really old.

Now the big 5-0 is upon you. How could that be? Why don't you feel old? Isn't there anything you can do — someone you can hire to fix this? Perhaps you should just ignore it, and go into hiding. You could become a conscientious objector against milestone birthdays. Or should you go to the other extreme and raise hell, drawing lots of attention to yourself?

But there's no hiding from 50, no matter how smart you are or how good looking you (still) are or how much money you made during the dot.com or real estate bubbles. And even though you know that 13,600 of your Boomer peers will turn 50 every day until the year 2015 (and that's just in North America), there's little comfort in these numbers. When it comes to turning 50, every one of us is on our own.

When Leslie, my significant other, turned 50, I decided to throw a huge bash for her to commemorate her 'passing.' I invited 150 of our friends, hired a ten-piece Salsa band complete with a horn section and two drummers, rolled up the rugs, and moved all of our living room furniture into the garage. For eight hot, sweaty, foundation-shaking hours we danced, ate, drank, and celebrated Leslie.

As the night progressed, I noticed that every 50-something guest felt obligated to pull Leslie aside and offer advice. The doctors named the tests and procedures she should have done. The lawyers (always the largest constituency at parties) advised her about tax and estate planning. The artists (who used to be the largest constituency at parties back in the 60s) recommended exhibits to see or specific masterpieces to view. The professors encouraged her to read specific books while the financial professionals scribbled stock tips on napkins and told her how to restructure her portfolio.

I am a publisher by trade, and in the midst of Leslie's raucous, jubilant, 50th birthday party, I realized that there was a tremendous amount of valuable information available. The problem was that no one had thought to gather it together into one book. The idea for *Fifty Things To Do When You Turn Fifty* was born.

The book that you are holding in your hands took three years to produce. The celebrities, artists, pundits, and business experts who were kind enough to contribute to it have provided a wealth of information. Their personal remembrances are funny, informative, and soothing — an instruction manual that is both useful and touching.

But as useful, enlightening, and (in many cases) funny as the various essays are, what I find I value most is the feeling of hope and optimism that comes through — a sense that everything will be okay.

I hope that you, too, will be left with this same feeling. I hope you will realize that although 50 is a threshold you pass through alone, there are many who have gone before you, ready to offer guidance. If you heed their advice, relax (you don't have to prove yourself any longer), take care of yourself, and remain inspired, you will have plenty to look forward to in the years ahead. Sure, you have to face 50 alone, but you're not in such bad company, after all. And once you muster the courage to pass through that doorway, you'll find lots of friendly faces waiting for you on the other side.

Ronnie Sellers

Section One

FINDING YOUR
50-SOMETHING
ATTITUDE

1

Stop complaining

**No one cares that you don't like getting older —
so quit bellyaching. But 50 is a great time to lose
the ponytail, start telling the truth, and stop having
dinner with people you don't like.**

BY GARRISON KEILLOR

Garrison Keillor is the host of *A Prairie Home Companion*,
which is heard Saturday nights on public radio stations
around the country. He lives in St. Paul, Minnesota.

When you hit 50, you have to stop complaining
about getting old, the strangeness of it, the fas-
cination, the horror, etc., etc. That was okay
in your 30s and 40s, but now that you're old, it's time
to shut up on the subject. The term "senior moment,"
for example, or joking references to your prostate or
Alzheimer's: Stifle it. You shouldn't complain about
aging for the simple reason that nobody gives a hoot. If
you were to pay people to care, they might care a little
bit for an hour or two, but you didn't and they don't. So

learn to be cheerful about it. When people ask how you are, tell them, "Absolutely great. Never better."

Fifty is the time to try giving up television and newspapers and radio for six months or a year and see what the simple, unmediated life of direct experience is like. You won't know if you don't try.

By 50, everyone can stand to lose 20 pounds, so do it. The simplest way is to adopt a new philosophy of eating, which is revolutionary in America but which is essential for an older person: Eat to satisfy hunger; if you're not hungry, don't eat. Stop eating when your hunger is satisfied. Except on Sunday or whichever day is your feast day. As you get older, your metabolism changes, and now you can sustain yourself quite well on one meal per day and two snacks. So that's what you do.

Fifty is the time to take a long, hard look in the mirror. Especially for the aging bohemian. A young person is allowed to dress up as Desperado, Punk Princess, Noir Poet, or Frontiersman, but by the age of 50 you've wised up. You've seen how ratty those old ponytails can look. What was revolutionary at 21 can be rather stringy and pitiful at 50. What works for Willie Nelson doesn't necessarily work for you. So you look at yourself and maybe you adopt a new look and do it in a totally cool way, no comment, no angst, just shave and shower and cut the hair short and drop some weight, start running, put on a jacket and tie, and if jaws drop, you just say, "Hey, why not?" You do not compromise your principles one degree, you don't tone down your views, you simply adopt a more conventional look, which might free you up in all sorts of ways.

Put the past behind you. This is even easier to do at my age (62) but you can get a start at 50 — make a pile of your regrets and put a match to them and let them blow away, the lost loves, the estranged friends, the botched education, the unwritten novel, the neglected guitar, the ruinous investments, the dear friend who committed suicide, the opportunities that sailed away without you — put that knapsack full of rocks on the ground and walk away and find something in the here-and-now that absorbs you and take up with that, a garden, a grandchild, a choir, yoga, knitting, amassing a collection of porcelain pigs, political agitation, learning the drop-thumb style of banjo.

Start telling the truth. In small doses at first and then gradually build up to one out of three, a decent batting average. When you're young, you're scared, you're trying to wend your way through the trees and not get shot at, you're trying to stay on the warm side of the various big cheeses in your life, you're wanting to be the good guy who everybody loves, not the jerk with the big mouth. But when you hit 50, you're entering a new passage of life in which you can say what you really think. You can express outrage at the shameful things that take place in this dear land, the shabby treatment of the poor and the young, the gorgeous favors bestowed on the rich, the swift growth of government under our conservative regime.

You can also dare to express simple preference. Do you want to go over to the Swansons' for dinner? No, I don't. Why not? I thought you liked them. They complain constantly about aging and I'm tired of looking at his hair. Oh. Okay. What would you rather do? Lie on a bed with you and talk and drink a little wine and listen to Frank Sinatra with the lights out. Oh. Okay.

Speaking of wine, 50 is also a good time to take an honest look at the beverages in your life. The miseries of alcohol are probably clear to you by now, and so you might, as an intellectual and spiritual exercise, take a vacation from booze and learn to appreciate the world's panoply of excellent teas. For most people, this will be a struggle, but there is something to be gained, and that is simplicity. If you worry about alcohol, then you probably have good reason to, and that is enough reason to take a vacation. Refrain for a month and that will make the next month easier and soon you'll be to six months and a year, and after that, it's not so hard: Not drinking is easy so long as you don't drink.

Fifty is an excellent age for reform of all sorts. You have enough experience and good judgment to know something about yourself and you can see the end of your life from here and so, gauging your desires and your strength, you adjust and straighten and balance and alter what needs altering and press on. It's a time of marvels on every hand, great richness, emotional clarity, and great sweetness. Sixty is even better, but don't hurry.

2

Look for what's hopeful and go with it

At 50, you've got plenty of reasons for optimism.

BY WENDY WASSERSTEIN

Wendy Wasserstein was one of the most influential writers and playwrights on Broadway. A native New Yorker she won the Pulitzer Prize and the Tony Award for her play, *The Heidi Chronicles.* Ms. Wasserstein died in January 2006.

I used to make lists at every decade birthday of what I wanted to do, what I felt I needed to accomplish. But I didn't make one when I turned 50. I think between 40 and 50, I learned a lot more about life. My oldest sister, Sandra, died of breast cancer when I was 47. My daughter, Lucy Jane, was born 10 weeks early when I was 49. So I sort of started seeing the ridiculousness of lists.

Not that lists are necessarily ridiculous in and of themselves. I know that you can plan some things. But you can't plan others.

And you begin to think about luck — what's lucky and what's not. That may be unfortunate because it means that I agree with my friend, playwright Christopher Durang, that life is random.

I didn't like turning 50 very much. I remember having a party when I turned 40, but also being very anxious, because my life had been so much more focused on my career than on my personal life. I thought, there's all this stuff I've still got to do. I've got to get a home, I have to have a child. Turning 50 was harder because my sister had died, and my Dad was sick. It just was harder — there was a lot of real life going on. With so much loss, it became about survival. Of course if your sister and your father and your best friend die, what are you supposed to do? It made me think, what's precious to me? What do I really care about?

By the time you're 50, certain things have less importance in your life in terms of aging, especially if you're a woman. Unless you're a movie star, unless you're used to being Cate Blanchett all your life (which would be a different thing; I'm sure that must be hard, too). If you're Wendy Wasserstein and you turn 50, it's not like you say,

"I really miss that figure." I just thought, "I am who I am. It's just fine." That was quite liberating.

And then the big question — what am I going to do when I grow up? There always seemed to be an endless amount of time to answer that. When you're 50, you know there isn't an endless amount of time. You just know it. But you still have to believe that you can change things. If you didn't believe you could change things, it would be horrible.

So you find things to get you through. You try to have a strong enough backbone. And you try not to get hysterical. A sense of humor is essential because it's not fake. Unless it's a laugh track on television — when someone says, "I'm crossing the street," and you hear laughter. Obviously there's no laugh track in life. If you're really funny, it means there's a lack of pretense, a sense of humanity. It's an understanding that you're not that important. "It" is not that important. Self-importance can be a dangerous thing.

At this juncture, I suppose some women feel that they're reborn and ready to go, with their family grown, and that they're entering into a wonderful third phase of their life. If you try to be positive, you have to think there are new things to learn. You get scared of becoming entrenched, not meeting new people and expanding in new ways. But what I've found most useful since I've turned 50 is that the things that I feel are deep in my life have gotten deeper. My friendships with the people I really like have become deeper. I'm much less interested in parties and connections. I feel much closer to my friends. I try to spend more time with my daughter. I'm closer to my work and the things I really care about. I've gone deeper into what's there.

I've said that I'm nice in a sometimes-rueful way. But now I think "nice" has gotten a bad connotation. I think nice is nice. Nice has gotten a bum rap as sort of not sexy, not edgy, not interesting. In fact, kindness can go a long way.

You have to decide there's hope. I think there's hope in acceptance, too. For instance, I wrote an article for *More* magazine about turning 50, saying that for a 50-year-old woman, hope comes with a lot of history, a degree of disappointment, some skepticism, and a great deal of depth. And as I've said before, you just have to show up every day and hope for the best. You do the best that you can — that is really how I feel about being 50. For someone turning 50, I would say — and this is in a new play of mine — "Go with the hope." Look for what's hopeful, and try to find that hope.

3

Write your own top ten list

You don't have to be David Letterman to come up with your own list of 10 great things about turning 50.

BY PATRICIA FARRELL, PH.D.

Patricia Farrell, Ph.D., is a licensed psychologist and a regular on such national TV shows as *The View*, *The Maury Show*, and *The O'Reilly Factor*. The native New Yorker is also the author of *How to Be Your Own Therapist* (McGraw-Hill). Dr. Farrell is also the expert for WebMD's Anxiety/ Panic Board.

Bette Davis said, "Old age is no place for sissies," and at 50, I've come to believe her. I've also come to believe that 50 is the new 30, at least as far as I'm concerned. The dread I recall when I was approaching my 30th birthday was clearly out of proportion to anything that actually happened on or after that fateful day. So when 50 rolled around, it was a piece of cake in every sense of the word. I was now firmly planted in adulthood and, clearly, my own person in my own career. Who would have thought?

Of course, we psychologists have a way of looking at most things, even the aging process, as positive rather than negative. So my birthday gift to you is to pass on some of that positive thinking to get you beyond any lingering anxiety you might have about this momentous age.

I'll do that with my own personal list of the top 10 positive things about turning 50. Read them carefully and you'll understand why I believe we should all view this milestone as a beginning of something new.

10. *You no longer have to worry about what your parents will say if you don't come home on time.* In fact, you don't even have to go home if you don't want to. The glorious part about turning 50 is that you're now into that part of your life in which the family "elders" can no longer make you feel anxious or guilty with their dire pronouncements about what you're doing (or not doing) with your life (you may even be the family elder). Today, what you do with your life is your responsibility — no one else's. If you want to, as they say, "go to hell in a hand basket," it's your choice.

9. *You can read whatever you want, whenever you want.* Be it trashy novels or literary classics, both feed your brain and enrich your life. You're old enough to know that now, so pig out at the bookstore and read what you want. No more hiding "trashy" books under your bed,

in the closet, or out in the garage. After all, you're 50 and your own person! Besides, you can tell them, studies show that reading helps stave off Alzheimer's disease. So let Danielle Steele, or any other writer you like, come to your cognitive rescue.

8. *Your financial life and financial future are in your hands.* You're the one earning the money and paying the bills. No more asking if you can go anywhere or buy anything. It's up to you to decide how good or bad you'll feel afterwards. Anyway, what's wrong with one of those delicious impulse purchases?

7. *You can eat anything you want for breakfast, be it birthday cake, cold pizza, Chinese food, or even souvlaki.* Breakfast, after all, is the most important meal of the day. That doesn't mean, however, that you have to observe the usual rules all the time. In fact, cereal for dinner also sounds good!

6. *You no longer have to worry about keeping up with what's current in music, and you can dance the way you want to.* Like the music of the '70s, '80s, or even the '40s? Let it rip and play it in your car, your home, or your office. As Barbra Streisand once said, "This is the only music that makes me dance." So dance away wherever or whenever you want.

5. *You no longer have to put on makeup (or hold your stomach in) before you put the garbage out.* It's okay for your neighbors, the garbage man, or anyone else to see that, indeed, you do not awaken as they do in film — fully made up.

4. *You can declare Sunday to be an absolute day of rest without guilt.* One of the perks of being a grown-up is spending the seventh day in bed with the newspapers, cookies, chocolate, or submarine sandwiches if you want. It's your day and you make the rules.

3. *You no longer have to consider golf a competitive sport.* By now, the game should just be fun. If other people don't realize that, it's up to you to educate them. In fact, at this time in your life, secondhand clubs are more fashionable than the latest technology because they show that you care not a whit for impressing any-one and that the game, not the trappings, is what's most important.

2. *You no longer have to adhere to some unrealistic idea of thinness.* Why diet until you fit into clothes that you deliberately bought too small? You know what's comfort-able and healthy, and you have the brains and the will to take care of yourself. Today's diet expert is tomorrow's has-been.

1. *You no longer have to answer that question we all hate: What are you going to be when you grow up?* You're all grown up now, and if you want to change careers, that's okay, too. No one can make you keep on doing something you absolutely hate.

It's also time to realize some of those long-held wishes. What will it be . . . a Hawaiian vacation? Skiing in the Rockies? Shopping for hidden treasures in those little out-of-the-way markets that dot the side roads of America? Stop wishing and start planning.

Enough words of wisdom from a psychologist? If not, here are a few more. The fact that you've reached 50 and are reading this book is a milestone in and of itself. It shows that you've done pretty well with your life up to this point. I urge you to continue seeking the joy in life and reframing the setbacks. Remember, whenever you're not sure if you should do something spontaneous, buy something frivolous, or say something silly, just tell yourself: "I've earned it!"

4

Find your inner elegy

The former Poet Laureate grapples with a dark night of the soul to see the light of 50.

BY BILLY COLLINS

Billy Collins served as the U.S. Poet Laureate for 2001-2003 and has won the Oscar Blumenthal Prize, the Levinson Prize, and a Guggenheim Foundation fellowship. His poems appear regularly in publications such as *The New Yorker*, *The Paris Review*, and *Harper's*. Collins has published more than seven volumes of poetry; his *Questions About Angels* won the National Poetry Series publication prize.

Poetry has as many subjects as there are things in the world around us, but the underlying subject of poetry, as every English major knows, is Death. In fact, students who decide to major in English should be advised that they are actually majoring in Death. So for poets, every day is a good day to write a poem on mortality, but the occasion of a birthday brings the subject into sharp focus, and if the birthday number ends in a

31

zero . . . well, poets are apt to feel a professional obligation to mark the event with some utterance in verse. The following is my response to turning 50, and the chilling thought of it, as the end of the poem makes clear, was enough to scare me back into the arms of the Church, or at least into the grip of her language.

Fiftieth Birthday Eve

The figure alone is enough to keep me wide awake,
the five with its little stationmaster's belly
and cap with the flat visor, followed by the zero,
oval of looking glass, porthole on a ghost ship,
an opening you stick your arm into and feel nothing.

I want to daydream here in the dark, listening
to the trees behind the house reciting their poems,
bare anonymous beings, murmuring to themselves
in lines that reach out like long branches in spring.
I want my mind to be a sail, susceptible to any breeze
that might be blowing across the lake of consciousness.

But I keep picturing the number, round and daunting:
I drop a fifty-dollar bill on a crowded street,
I carry a fifty-pound bag of wet sand on my shoulders.
I see fifty yearlings leaping a fence in a field,
I fan the five decades before me like a poker hand.

I try contemplating the sufferings of others, Rossini,

for example, considered by many to be the Father
of Modern Insomnia for his prolonged sleeplessness
during the composition of the *William Tell Overture.*

But even a long meditation on the life of Brahms,
widely recognized as the Father of the Modern Lullaby,
will not dispel the fives and zeros, gnomes in the night
perched on the bedposts, one straddling a closet
doorknob.

By dawn, I have become a Catholic again,
the oldest altar boy in the parish, complete
with surplice and cassock, cruet, thurible, and candle.

And this day, whose first light is gilding the windows,
has become another one of the sorrowful mysteries,
following the agony in the garden of childhood
and preceding the crucifixion,
the letter X removed from the word
and nailed to a cross,

the rest of the alphabet standing witness
on the rocky hillside, marveling at the lightning
that is cutting silently across the dark sky.

5

Keep a sense of adventure

**At midlife, most of us face a fork in the road.
It's up to us to decide whether to take the easy ride,
or the uncertain one to spiritual rebirth.**

BY MARIANNE WILLIAMSON

Marianne Williamson has published eight books, four of
which have reached No. 1 on *The New York Times* best seller
list, including *A Return to Love* and *Everyday Grace*. Other
works include *Illuminata*, *A Woman's Worth*, and *Healing the
Soul of America*.

I found turning 50 harder than I expected it to be.
Somewhere around two or three months before the
big day, I started to be haunted by memories of a
youth now irrevocably over. As much as I told myself that
50 is the new 40, what I really wanted in my heart was to
have the old 40 back. I had waking nightmares of blaz-
ing memories — things I hadn't handled well, stupid
choices I had made and could not make over, chances I
thought were never more to be retrieved. Grieving the

glory of my younger years, I had to face myself and all the pain that comes with that.

Several friends told me they had experienced the same thing, but not to worry — all of a sudden the anxiety would lift. And indeed that is the way it happened for me. Sitting at an outside cafe late on the night of my big 5-0, looking up at the Eiffel Tower lit up against the sky, I felt the pain lift. In an instant, it was all okay. I knew the sun had set on what was no longer, but I had a sense that something new would now dawn to take its place.

Girlfriends had told me that the 50s are great because you don't care anymore what others think. I don't know if that will be true for me, but I do know that I'm not who I used to be. Fifty is as different from 40 as 40 is from 30 and 30 from 20. With the coming of 50, one makes a transition as fundamental as that of puberty. I have settled into the paradox of middle age.

On one hand, you finally have some sense of what you're doing in the world. At last I'm convinced I have a right to be here. I'm not as frantic as I used to be, though I can't tell yet whether that's because I've evolved or just aged. On the other hand, I get tired more easily, I often can't remember things, and I'm exhausted just from looking for my glasses all the time! Most disconcerting of all, when I'm in a serious mood and I do the math,

I can't garner much hope of changing things on this planet during the time I have left. Our generation's shared delusion that we would usher in paradise has been completely shattered. The older you get, the more you see how entrenched certain negatives are. There is so much cruelty in the world that you thought for years would go away; and as you age, it dawns on you that it never really does.

As disillusioning as it is to realize these things — and disillusionment is actually a good thing because it means you were laboring under illusions before — it's also the beginning of spiritual insight. Once you're deeply convinced there are no ultimate answers outside yourself, you start looking for them where they truly are: inside. And you realize that in your slowing down, you're more prepared to listen to things you were moving too fast to hear before.

So much wasted time, so many stupid mistakes. You feel you have the knowledge now, but you're not sure you have the energy left: If only you had known then what you know now. You come to understand George Bernard Shaw's comment, "Youth is wasted on the young."

Our adrenal glands decimated, our cells like fast cars beginning to show wear, the fastest generation has begun to slow down. Jack Nicholson said in a recent interview, "My generation is the new old." Our deepest burden is the accumulated sorrow, the heartbreak of one decade impinging upon the next until the heart can absorb no more. Your mind has figured so much out, but your body isn't sure that it cares anymore. When it's more depressing than joyful to wake up in the morning, then you know you have a problem.

And many people do.

Most people, once they hit middle age, face a fork in the road. And which road they take, in the words of Robert Frost, will make all the difference. One road leads to gradual dissolution — a cruise however slow toward death. The other road becomes a birth canal, a pattern of spiritual rebirth. The older we get, the harder it is to choose rebirth. The ego's gravity seems harder to resist.

We start out so enthusiastic about life, so entertained and delighted by the very nature of things. But the newness fades; we grow jaded or exhausted, and we begin to lose some vital appreciation for the possibilities inherent in a day. As I write this, I hear teenagers in my backyard, delighting in the mud puddles produced by the afternoon's storm. I have to consciously check myself — to remind myself that the ability to have fun in the mud is what makes being young so wonderful, and not make a stink about the fact that my towels are beige and this could ruin them. My mortal truth is that I want the kids to hose off before they come back into the house, but my soul's truth is that I wish I could enjoy the mud too.

So it's completely up to me, whether I start to become an old biddy who cares too much about the towels, or instead hold onto my sense of adventure and remember what's important. What the hell, the kids are happy and that is what's important. And not just for kids, but for all of us.

Section Two

MAKING PEACE
WITH THE MIRROR

6

Stop obsessing about your flaws

The only beauty secret that matters is learning to look more like you, and less like somebody else.

BY BOBBI BROWN

Bobbi Brown, the founder and CEO of Bobbi Brown Cosmetics, was working as a makeup artist in New York when she launched her company — with just 10 brown-based lipsticks — in 1991. These quickly gained a strong following first among beauty insiders, then women everywhere.

As I look to turning 50, I can finally say that I've come to terms with myself, and I hope the things I've learned along the way will help other women see their own beauty.

When I was 13 years old, I wanted to look like Cheryl Tiegs. She was tall, thin, and blonde — the epitome of beauty in the late 1960s. Standing at just five feet tall, with dark brown eyes, dark brown hair, and strong eyebrows, I couldn't have looked any more different. I spent a lot of time feeling bad about this until I saw Ali MacGraw in *Love Story*. Those dark eyes, that hair, and those thick eyebrows . . . in her I finally saw the possibility of my own beauty. This realization changed how I viewed myself, how I saw other women, and it ultimately led me to my career as a makeup artist.

My love and obsession with makeup began at age six when my mother gave me a box of her old cosmetics, a pad of paper, and the instructions to have fun drawing while she prepared dinner. Instead, I chose to make up all my dolls and stuffed animals to perfection. At 16, I landed my first job at a small makeup boutique. As part of my orientation, the owner gave me a makeover to "correct" what she saw as my flaws. She applied pink foundation to cover my too-yellow skin; shaded my nose to make it look smaller; tweezed my brows into thin, sparse lines; and outlined my lips outside my natural lip line to "create fullness." I couldn't wait to go home to wash my face when I saw my reflection in the mirror.

When I look at a woman, I don't see what's wrong with her, I see what's right — and that's why I'm troubled by the current definition of beauty that favors a cosmetic surgery-enhanced, cookie-cutter look. Women who look like the ones I grew up admiring (women like my grandmother, Helen Hayes, and Jessica Tandy) are nowhere to be found. Who's to blame for this? We all are. Magazines, billboards, TV shows, and movies are filled with images of preternaturally youthful, impossibly proportioned women.

We have a choice. We can buy into these images or we can make the conscious decision not to. True beauty isn't about looking like a supermodel (remember, they're freaks of nature) or a 20-something Barbie doll (what does the woman who created Barbie look like anyway?). True beauty is about accepting and feeling good about who you are. Here are some of the things to do as you approach your 50th birthday:

• *Stop obsessing.* Instead of stewing over your "flaws" and the things you don't like about yourself, look at what's right. I can't tell you how many times women come to my makeup counter so fixated on the size and shape of one feature that they overlook everything else. When a woman asks me how to make her nose appear smaller, I point out her amazing smile and show her how to enhance her lips with the right lipstick and gloss. More often than not, she is pleasantly surprised by what she sees.

• *Live in the present.* We spend a lot of energy wanting to recapture what we used to look like, instead of appreciating where we currently are. I hated my arms when I was a teenager and often wore long-sleeved shirts. Now

I look back on pictures from those days and I think that my arms looked just fine. I would have saved myself a lot of adolescent angst if I had made the best of what I had at the time.

• *Be who you are.* This means everything from learning to love the lines in your face to appreciating your own unique features. There's something incredibly beautiful about a woman with lines in her face, and I think we should start using the word "living" instead of "aging." Facial lines are hard-earned proof that you've lived a rich, emotion-filled life. Take them all away and you end up looking like a blank, plastic-faced mannequin. Tip: A little concealer and the right blush do wonders.

• *Take charge of yourself.* Instead of fighting the body you have, accept it and make the most out of it. Focus on being healthy, strong, and fit. Commit to making smart food choices and exercising regularly. Yes, this requires work and it's not a quick fix, but you'll look and feel better over the long term. I'm 47 years old and I'm still learning that there's a lot I can do to be the best version of myself.

We've all heard the adage "beauty is only skin deep." Well, it's high time we proved it wrong. Beauty goes far beyond the physical and what you see in the mirror. It begins from within and it's all about self-confidence. That's something that no doctor can prescribe.

7

Put your best face forward

Just because you accept yourself doesn't mean you can't spruce up a few things. And now is a good time for a little nip-and-tuck prevention.

BY VALERIE J. ABLAZA, M.D., FACS

Valerie Ablaza is a Board Certified plastic surgeon and is a partner in The Plastic Surgery Group in Montclair, New Jersey. She received her medical degree from The Medical College of Pennsylvania, completed her residency in plastic surgery at The New York Hospital-Cornell Medical Center, is a fellow of the American College of Surgeons, and is a member of the American Society of Plastic Surgeons.

Have you recently walked by a mirror and thought you saw your mother's image out of the corner of your eye? Do you find yourself wearing turtlenecks more often? Do you stand in front of the mirror and push your breasts up or put your hands on the sides of your face and push backwards? Answer "yes" to any of these questions and maybe it's time to add "talk to cosmetic surgeon" to your to-do list. I often hear people say that they just want their external appearance to match the way they feel on the inside. And inside, they feel oh, about 30 . . . not 50! That's my job: to help turn back the hands of time.

You might think those wrinkles, jowls, turkey neck, and extra inches have developed almost overnight, but I assure you the changes have been steadily, albeit slowly, evolving since about your 35th birthday. The signs are subtle, but clear. Mornings when you look like you've pulled an all-nighter, even though you slept like a baby. People commenting on how angry you look all the time — when you're in a perfectly good mood. Love handles, droopy bellies, and sagging thighs, even though you're the same weight you've been for the past 10 years. And breasts that have taken a decided slide southward!

I've also noticed a direct correlation between the amount of liquid makeup and concealer women use and their eagerness to get an appointment with me. It's that time of life when the same amount of makeup just doesn't give the same results. Witch hazel on cotton balls doesn't work for puffy eyelids as it did in college!

And men, don't think that you've completely dodged the curve ball. Your face, with the aging changes that have made you eligible for that "Most Distinguished Look" award, can also be refreshed with a number of cosmetic procedures. Take heart — there's even a solution for the love handles, spare tires, and unwanted fatty deposits that have "suddenly appeared" in your breast area.

That's right. Cosmetic plastic surgery is not just for women. You may be surprised to know that men represent almost 20 percent of those opting for cosmetic procedures as a way to deal with image maintenance and change.

"Wait!" you're thinking. "I'm not old enough for plastic surgery! Isn't that for really old people?" Hardly. After all, why wait until your face looks like melting wax before doing something about it? It's so much better to begin with subtle, relatively simple fixes today that will keep you looking good longer without dramatically altering your appearance. Think of such procedures more as a "make-better" and less as a "make-over." The goal of cosmetic procedures today isn't to turn you into someone else; it's to keep you looking just like yourself — only a younger, more refreshed, more relaxed version.

The old days when cosmetic plastic surgery was reserved for the very wealthy with lots of time on their hands are over. Today, anyone with a few hundred dollars can get a lunchtime facial peel, a Botox injection, or a quick laser procedure. Even a face-lift can be done in less time and with more natural-looking results (no more "wind tunnel" effect) than in years past.

And the options . . . Oh, there are so many for both men and women to enjoy!

How about an eyelid lift to remove excess skin and fat pockets on your upper and lower eyelids and raise the corners of your drooping eyes? A neck lift to restore a youthful jaw line and improve the sagging angle of your neck? A face-lift not only to tighten the skin on your face but also to reposition sinking cheeks, minimize jowls, and give a boost to the corners of your mouth?

Happy with your face? Well, what about your chest, stomach, and thighs? Liposuction is great for removing unwanted fat on a man's chest as well as for getting rid of excess fat from the abdomen, hips, and thighs of both men and women. And if loose skin is the problem, tummies can be "tucked," and breasts and thighs can be "lifted." Push-up bras and girdles will become a distant memory. But you don't have to go the full surgical route. Botox not only minimizes forehead creases, crow's feet and other wrinkles; it can also give a little lift to your eyebrows. Injectable materials including fat, Restylane, Juvederm and Radiesse can fill in hollow areas and soften those hard-earned "character lines," while microdermabrasion, chemical peels, and laser resurfacing can help rejuvenate skin that had, maybe, a touch too much sun three decades ago.

How about permanent makeup to enhance fading lip color and avoid lipstick "bleeding" into the small vertical lines on the edges of your lips and corners of your mouth? And anyone who has become a victim of "short-arm syndrome" will appreciate not having to apply eyeliner or pencil in thinning eyebrows ever again.

So if your spouse, significant other, friends, or family members have run out of "perfect gifts" for your 50th birthday, drop a little hint for a gift certificate for a plastic surgery evaluation or, even better, for a rejuvenation procedure. If they're not getting the hint, give yourself this perfect gift. There's nothing wrong with making changes to help you feel better about yourself!

8

Wear comfortable clothes

The only way to be beautiful is to feel at ease.

BY DIANE VON FURSTENBERG

Belgian-born fashion designer Diane Von Furstenberg is best known for creating the wrap dress in the 1970s while she was still in her 20s. In her 50s, she has reinvented herself and her business to become one of the first major fashion figures to sell on QVC — and make it cool. Today, Von Furstenberg designs everything from swimwear to cell phones to costumes for an independent feature film she helped produce in 2005 called *Forty Shades of Blue.*

I can't pretend to be any other age, because I live my life so intensely. At 50, I couldn't have lied and said that I was 45 because I had lived those extra five years. From the minute I wake in the morning, I live very fully. I do so much in a day; I do so much in a week — I can't pretend that I haven't done it. I am my age. It would be silly to pretend that I am younger.

My 50s have been excellent. I have a huge amount of energy, and my experiences have been phenomenal.

When I was only 28, I had 300 people working for me; I was on the cover of *Newsweek*. But even when I was 20, I was thinking about 30. I enjoyed my 30s too, but in my 40s, I made some serious changes. I sold my business. I did not work. I fell in love. But work is good for me. I love to work. I had created a brand that was like a child to me. I had a son and a daughter and a brand. Then I lost my brand — it had deteriorated. So 50 marked the beginning of a period of rejuvenation.

When I was very young, I lived like an old person. I lived on Fifth Avenue at the Carlyle Hotel, and I enjoyed that. But when I turned 50, I was too old to live like an old person, so I moved downtown. I took some major steps going into my 50s: I restarted my business; I bought a new office building, and I restarted my clothing line — just as I had the first time around.

My company is now seven years old and it's successful, very trendy, and very young. I am surrounded by young people. Anyone working with me could be my daughter. The idea that young people think that I'm hip, and the fact that I dress young people, is very rejuvenating to me. It makes me feel good. Always being with young people is my way of staying youthful.

Adjusting your style to fit a particular age is a slightly foreign concept to me. I don't think, for instance, that at one particular age you can wear white, and then at a later age, you go black, and between the two all you have are shades of gray. In the intimacy of a fitting room, in a bathroom, all women are the same. I think there are no rules.

Well, perhaps there is one rule: I believe that people have to be comfortable. The most important thing that makes a woman feel attractive is being confident; in order to feel confident you have to wear clothes that are comfortable and that you feel make you look better. But ultimately, you just have to live your life and not think too much about it. It's always painful when you see people who are too constricted, forcing themselves into something that even they on a certain level feel they don't belong in. If a woman is at ease, she'll look beautiful.

There are a multitude of clothing choices for women. I never recommend anything for a woman specifically because of her age or because she's a blonde, or some other statistic. The primary factor is that it's all about who she is. It's about enjoying who you are and becoming more and more comfortable with who you are. Since you are going to live in your own skin your whole life, the sooner you are comfortable with it, the better. As the years go by, you are the one who knows all your secrets, all your complexities. You know your experience. You may as well have a good relationship with yourself.

You live your life and you grow into your life and you have small children, then you have big children. And then you have grandchildren, and you are still the same person; the important thing is to keep yourself agile in body and brain. Pay attention, be curious, be engaged, and live.

Just enjoy it. You may think 50 is old, but three years from now you will think it is young. That's one very positive aspect of thinking ahead. ☀

Thanks to David Moin, editor of *Woman's Wear Daily*, for his assistance with this piece.

9

Take your self back

Escaping the beauty trap isn't easy. You can regain the humor, the intensity, and the balance you had in childhood. It's worth it!

BY ERICA JONG

Erica Jong is an award-winning poet, essayist, and best-selling novelist. She is the author of *Fear of Flying, How to Save Your Own Life, Fanny: Being the True History of the Adventures of Fanny Hackabout-Jones, Parachutes & Kisses, Shylock's Daughter, Any Woman's Blues,* and *Inventing Memory: A Novel of Mothers and Daughters,* among others.

At 50, the last thing I wanted was a public celebration. Three days before my birthday, I took off for a spa in the Berkshires with Molly (then 13) — slept in the same bed with her, giggling before sleep, slumber party style — worked out all day (as if I were a jock, not a couch potato), learned trendy low-fat vegetarian recipes, had my blackheads expunged, my flab massaged, my muscles stretched, and thought about the second half of my life.

These thoughts alternated between terror and acceptance. Turning 50, I thought, is like flying: hours of boredom, punctuated by moments of sheer terror.

When, on the evening of my birthday, my husband (who shares the same birthday but is one year older) arrived, I had to adjust to the disruption of my woman's world. He liked the food, but wisecracked about the holistic hokum. His critical-satirical male eye did not quite ruin my retreat, but somehow tainted it. I was doing inner work in the guise of outer exercise, and his presence made that inner work harder.

Real men don't like spas.

The year before, when he turned 50, I had made a party for him. I sent out invitations that read:

He's 50.
She's not.
Come help celebrate.

I still couldn't face 50 so I knew I did not want him to reciprocate for my 50th birthday. Nor did I want to do what Gloria Steinem had done: make a public benefit, raise money for women, and rise resplendent in an evening gown, shoulders dusted with glitter — as Gloria's lovely shoulders were — and say: "This is what 50 looks like."

Who can fail to admire such brave affirmation of older women? But I veered between wanting to change the date on my *Who's Who* entry and wanting to move to Vermont and take up organic gardening in drawstring pants and Birkenstocks.

I needed something private, female, and contemplative to sort out these conflicting feelings. A spa was perfect. And my daughter was the perfect companion — despite her adolescent riffing that spares no one, her mother least of all. Still there is something about a woman turning 50 that is female work, mother-daughter work, not to be shared with the whole male world — or even with those representatives of it whom one loves and cherishes.

My husband and I have always made much of our birthday — in part because we share it, and because, having met in midlife, after the wreckage of many relationships, we treasure the synchronicity of our births. But 50 is different for a woman than it is for a man. Fifty is a more radical kind of passage to the other side of life and this was something we could not share. Let him make fun of "new age" contemplation. I needed it, as have women back to antiquity. Venus de Milo contemplates herself turning into the Venus of Willendorf — if she doesn't watch out.

You tell yourself you ought to be beyond vanity. You read feminist books and contemplate falling in love with Alice B. Toklas. But years of brainwashing are not so easy to forget. The beauty trap is deeper than you thought. It's not so much the external pressures as the internal ones that bind. You cannot imagine yourself middle-aged, cute little you who always had "it" even when overweight.

And then there are eternal questions of love and sex: Can there be friendship between men and women as long as the hormones rage and rule? How is sex related to love — and love to sex? Are we truly pigeonholed in our sexuality — or does society alone insist on this? What is "straight"? What is "gay"? What is "bi"? And does any of it matter deep in one's soul? Shouldn't we get rid of these labels in an attempt to be really open to ourselves and to each other?

What was happening to me in the second part of my life? I was getting myself back and I liked that self. I was getting the humor, the intensity, the balance I had known in childhood. But I was getting it back with a dividend. Call it serenity. Call it wisdom. I knew what mattered and what did not. Love mattered. Instant orgasm did not.

Often I have tricked myself into writing with candor by telling myself I would not publish (or would publish only under a pseudonym — perhaps even a male pseudonym). Later, I might be persuaded to sign the book by the loving letters I received from readers or by the publisher's need for a brand name. But during the writing process, I could be free, could knock the censor — my mother? my grandmother? — off my shoulder only by promising myself never to let my words see publication. I wrote *Fear of Flying* that way and many subsequent books. Writing has often been accompanied by terror, silences, and then wild bursts of private laughter that suddenly make all the dread seem worthwhile.

But the great compensation for being 50 in a culture that is not kind to older women is that you are less about criticism and you are less afraid of confrontation. In a world not made for women, criticism and ridicule follow us all the days of our lives. Usually, they are indications that we are doing something right.

Is 50 too young to start an autobiography? Of course it is. But maybe 80 is too old.

Fifty is the time when time itself begins to seem short . . . At 19, at 29, at 39, even — goddess help me — at 49, I believed that a new man, a new love, a move, a change to another city, another country, would somehow change my inner life.

Not so now.

I know that my inner life is my own achievement whether there is a partner in my life or not. I know that another mad, passionate love affair would be only a temporary distraction — even if "temporary" means two or three years. I know that my soul is what I have to nurture and develop and, alone or with a partner, the problems of climbing your own mountain are not so very different.

In a relationship, you still require autonomy, separateness, privacy. Outside, you still need self-love and self-esteem.

I write this from a place of self-acceptance, cleansing anger, and raucous laughter. I am old enough to know that laughter, not anger, is the true revelation. I make the assumption that I am not so different from you.

Section Three

REDEFINING FITNESS

10

Take a Hike

Walking is tame; hiking is an adventure: Get close to nature, close to the sky, close to yourself.

BY KRISTINA HURRELL

Kristina Hurrell has been taking people to "greater heights" since 1988, first with Global Fitness Adventures and now SpaFari, a hiking spa that rejuvenates body, mind, and soul in "paradise on earth" locations around the globe. She lives in Snowmass, Colorado.

My motto for living is this: Climb to the highest of places — whether that be within or without (or both) — and discover all you can be. Stride through life with spirit and strength. Hike for health, happiness, and harmony. The determination that takes you up a mountain will take you through life. I've had the opportunity to hike the world's most beautiful trails for more than 20 years now and I'm happy to say that I have the same slim, toned, youthful figure of my early 30s.

My complexion glows (thanks also to nutrition and sun-protective hiking clothing) and, in celebrating my 50s, I can truly say I feel wonderful.

My love of motion began some 30 years ago with daily beach jogs in Malibu. I started with around a mile per day and built up to running marathons and training with the Santa Monica track club. But it was in 1985, when I became physical director of a world-famous boot-camp spa that I seriously fell in love with hiking. My enthusiasm for the sport soared when a neighbor who taught face-lifting exercises pointed out that long periods of running created a downward pull on the facial muscles. Not so with hiking! I was hooked, especially when the endorphin rush that I received — and craved — from running was just as easily attainable when I pump-hiked up a hill or mountain, without the added stress that running caused.

Hiking offers adventure. It costs nothing and fits into any schedule at virtually any time of the year. Be it on a tree-lined street, a park, a beach, or best of all, a wilderness trail that winds you uphill, hiking is a thrill for the senses. In fact, one of the sport's simplest but most profound pleasures is to pump-hike up a breathtaking (literally!) mountain trail, experience the exhilaration of reaching the top, then drink in the view.

Hiking can be addictive. Even traversing the same path a number of times offers new and different experiences. Regular hiking transforms jiggling flesh into firm, defined muscle in a matter of weeks; cardiovascular-fitness levels improve; circulation and skin tone are rejuvenated; and the sport is a useful tool for combating stress and fatigue. If you're distressed about anything . . . take a hike, alone. I guarantee it will bring you back to yourself and give you clarity.

Literally hundreds of my clients say that their quality of life has improved from regular hiking, people like Georgie Ducas, a 58-year-old novice hiker, who told me, "I've gained a lot of 'I can do it' self-confidence through mountain hiking. It's the best investment in my life I've ever made."

Hiking improves eye-foot coordination and dexterity, and it's great for developing balance. Just be aware of the nitty-gritty aspects of safe hiking. To begin, don't plod along by slumping or slouching and don't focus on the ground right in front of you — that's only necessary if the terrain is precarious.

Walk tall. Lift your crown and sternum. It's a cross between an assertive march and fluid loopy stride (think jaunty African Masai, loping through the bush). Don't be shy about pumping your arms — leg strength works in conjunction with good arm action. In addition, movement above the waist helps increase cardiovascular activity. Master the art of breathing: For horizontal terrain, breathe in for four strides and breathe out for four. For uphill hiking, breathe in deeply for two steps and out for two. Facial muscles, as well as neck and shoulders, should be relaxed.

Stay within your comfort zone by keeping your exercise heart rate to between 70 to 80 percent of your maximum capacity and strengthen it with short, anaerobic bursts. (It's okay to feel a little breathless, but you should be able to talk without gasping for air.)

Alternate your gaze between the far horizon, middle range, and close range — changing your focus works the eye muscles and keeps them healthy, plus it ensures that your eyes are really open to the beauty that surrounds you. When hiking downhill on slippery mud or shale rock, tuck in your tailbone to keep your spine straight, and take smaller, lighter steps. Try using hiking poles for extra security.

Proper hydration is essential. A good rule is to drink about a liter every two hours — the higher the altitude, the more you need. Pay attention to what your body tells you; higher altitudes can cause headache, fatigue, shortness of breath, dizziness, or nausea. These symptoms usually disappear after you adjust to the lower oxygen levels. The key is good hydration and deep breathing.

If you're planning a long hike, you'll need a backpack with a padded waist strap and chest cinch. The padded waist strap should comfortably distribute the backpack weight to your hips, not your shoulders. Contents should include water, rain jacket/pants, thermal top, bandana, medical kit, sunscreen, bug repellant, flashlight, whistle, cell phone (it might work in the mountains, you never know), compass/map, camera, notepad/pen, four zip-lock bags, tissues/wipes, and a warm hat and gloves. Wear well-fitting boots with ankle support and treaded soles, hiking socks, and sun protective shirt, pants, and gloves (for sun-sensitive skin), and a wide-brim sun hat with cinch. Keep a dry set of clothes and shoes in the car.

Remember always to respect the wilderness. It's offering you a wonderful opportunity; it's your job to help keep it that way, for yourself and others. Stay on the trail and leave nothing behind. Pack up your trash (including any used toilet paper, in the zip-lock bag). If you talk, keep your voice low so you can hear the music of nature. Try to be present in the moment. Immerse yourself in nature's artwork and let the awe-inspiring scenery uplift your soul. And to master any stressful thoughts, just say, "Go away . . . I'm hiking now!"

Take deep breaths and look around you . . . really *see*, from your innermost being, the flowers, earth, rocks, trees, and sky, the variety of colors, the light that dances on rivers, lakes, leaves, snow, or sea . . . and let that "light" dance inside of you. ☼

11

Limber up. Get flex-y with it.

Whether you're a couch potato or a seasoned athlete, yoga can free your body in ways you never dreamed possible.

BY JONATHAN FIELDS

Jonathan Fields is a dad, a husband, an entrepreneur, a founder/director of Sonic Yoga in New York City, a health and fitness industry guru, author of *Career Renegade: How to Make a Great Living Doing What You Love* (Broadway Books, 2009), an all-around marketing whiz, and a recovering hedge fund/securities lawyer. Visit his Web site jonathanfields.com.

Feeling a little achy as you head toward the half-century mark? Waking up several times in the night? Having trouble falling asleep? How's your blood pressure? Stress level? Self-image? The wear and tear of the first 50 years of life on our bodies threatens to make the next 50 less than ideal.

But give me about three hours of your time a week, and I can guarantee you'll feel better.

No, it's not a pill, not a therapy, not a procedure. It's yoga, an ancient Eastern practice now being recognized as an outstanding adjunct to modern medicine in terms of keeping you fit, healthy, and centered.

If you're like most Americans, though, yoga conjures up visions of double-jointed 20-somethings putting themselves into impossible positions and chanting. I've got news for you. Yoga today is about as mainstream as apple pie. Even small, rural communities have yoga classes, and in large cities they're as ubiquitous as dry cleaners. Plus, given all those health benefits, your doctor may even prescribe it for you!

So come along with me as I give you three user-friendly answers to three fairly giant questions: What is this thing called yoga? Why do I absolutely need it in my life? And, most important, how do I begin?

What is Yoga?

Asking a yoga teacher what yoga is is a bit like asking a physicist what space is, but here's my best shot. Yoga is both a system of daily practices and a philosophy of living that originated some 5,000 years ago to liberate people from suffering and unify them with their true "selves" (a.k.a. "enlightenment"). Classically, enlightenment is the end to the yoga means.

The reality, though, is that most people begin yoga with the more accessible daily physical practices in search of simply feeling better, stronger, and calmer.

There are many different schools and styles of yoga, but all have certain common elements, including the use of postures, breathing exercises, and meditation. Postures are practiced to strengthen, cleanse, and heal the body. Breathing exercises deepen the cleansing effect and help balance energy in the body. And meditation is amazingly powerful at quieting the mind and bringing you back to center.

Why Do I Absolutely Need Yoga in My Life?

Yoga is the ultimate one-stop lifestyle solution!
It can help:

- Reduce stress and manage both depression and blood pressure.
- Strengthen every muscle in your body.
- Burn calories (certain styles of yoga) and manage or lose weight.
- Improve your flexibility and ability to do more in life.
- Promote good posture and decrease back pain.
- Enhance concentration, clarity, and mental focus.

- Improve balance, both on and off the mat.
- Add something fun and joyous to your day.
- Increase your confidence and creativity.
- Help you sleep better and longer.
- Provide a great community of friends.

OK, I Get It. How Do I Begin?

Starting with an introductory workshop or program that teaches the basic postures in an interactive format is a great idea, but choosing your particular flavor of yoga can be confusing. Here are brief descriptions of the major types:

• *Iyengar* — High-level of attention to precision alignment, use of props, long holds. Best for those seeking therapeutic results or treatment of specific conditions.

• *Vinyasa/power yoga* — Students "flow" from one pose to the next in a dance-like rhythm, tied to the breath. Dynamic and often challenging.

• *Ashtanga* — Similar to vinyasa/power yoga, but usually refers to a specific, fixed sequence of very physical and dynamic postures that are held for a shorter time.

• *Restorative* — Gentle, supported poses with lots of attention to individual needs. Good for those recovering from injury or illness.

• *Hatha* — This term has come to signify a gentler, more centering approach to the practice of postures.

• *Anusara* — Similar to iyengar, emphasizes alignment and precision with a bit more flow.

• *Kundalini* — Emphasizes breathwork, freestyle movement, and student interaction.

• *Integral* — A gentle posture practice with strong grounding in breath, meditation, and study.

If it is within your means, working with a private teacher is a very powerful way to study. But for most of us, classes are a more realistic option. They are a great way to explore the many forms of yoga to see which type works best for you. It is always a good idea to begin with a gentle approach and then move to a more intense practice.

Chanting, in yoga, can be very intimidating for people who are new to the practice. Chanting is not about religion, but about community and a universal sense of spirituality. If you're not comfortable, it's fine to sit in silence; many types of classes don't include any chanting at all. But give it a try first; I can't tell you how many students have told me that they were terrified of chanting at first, but now love it.

Most importantly, as you begin your exploration, take a long-term perspective and move into it with a sense of humor and lightness. You may stumble along the path to a far more fulfilled place in your world. And, just as important, you will feel — physically and emotionally — much better!

Namaste (The light in me honors the light in you).

12

Indulge yourself in a playground fantasy

Want to transform from schlumpy to powerful?
Just act out your playground daydreams, from the
trapeze to the tango.

BY LUIS SANTEIRO

Luis Santeiro is a long-time writer of *Sesame Street*, for which
he has received fourteen Emmy Awards. He was also head
writer of the first bilingual sitcom, *Que Pasa, U.S.A.?*, which
aired on PBS and earned him another Emmy. His theatre
work includes *The Lady from Havana, A Royal Affair, Our Lady
of the Tortilla, Praying with the Enemy, The Rooster and the Egg,
Mixed Blessings*, and the musical *Barrio Babies*, which won
both the Richard Rodgers and Edward Kleban awards. He
recently completed his first novel, *Dancing with Dictators*.

Turning 50 means the time has finally come to do
that one thing you always said you wanted to do
but never got around to doing. You've bored family and friends with it for years, so this is it. There's no
putting it off one more day.

In my case, that itching fantasy was to swing from a trapeze — and I don't mean any old playground trapeze. I had dreamt of climbing one of those long center-ring rope ladders to some high-up platform, from which I would then leap and do fancy twirls in midair. Even my one-page kindergarten biography, which a farsighted teacher had compiled, attested to this longing. Under the heading of "professional aspiration" it spelled out in green ink, highlighted by splotches of glitter: circus trapeze artist.

A few days before my half-century anniversary I decided that I would spend part of it fulfilling that old nagging yen, so I called my local trapeze school and booked myself into a beginner's class. Now, I like to think that I've tried my best to keep fit through the years, but in doing so, I've also learned that no matter how much one tries to ward off the march of time, there's no avoiding looking pretty much whatever age you are. If you're 50 and someone says you look great, it's never because they think you're 30 — which turned out to be about the top age among my aerialist classmates.

As we formed a circle to listen to instructions, I noticed a couple of amused glances aimed in my direction, but I did not let that faze me. In fact, I secretly gloated when only moments later some of those cocky young cynics struggled clumsily up the unsteady rope ladder.

Then my turn came. By now I had decided to turn this into "The Battle of the Generations." So I took it slowly and deliberately, and surprising even myself, did it as if I'd been doing it my whole life. But then I reached my longed-for platform. As the instructor hitched me to a safety harness, I looked down and saw the net way below — and my palms began to sweat. "Oh, well," I thought, "my little birthday celebration tonight may have to be held in an emergency ward."

The first jump was the worst. The trapeze bar was much heavier than I ever imagined, and for an instant, when I took hold of it, I cursed my adventuresome stupidity. But then the instructor shouted "Hut!" and there was no more time for self-reproach. I had a choreographed move to perform with each subsequent "hut" that he uttered: Hook legs up through trapeze bar, let go of hands, swing forward, swing back, grab the bar again, unhook legs, and finally — let go and drop down into the net. Feeling the scratchy nylon mesh against my cheek gave me a wonderful sense of comfort and relief. "You did it!" I said to myself. Then I heard the instructor shout, "Okay, I think you're ready to try a two-handed catch!" I thought he was joking, but by now my adrenaline was flowing so freely that I was ready to try anything.

The two-handed catch actually turned out to be simpler than one would imagine — at least for the student.

Once you have mastered the basic moves, all you have to do is hang head down, swing forward, extend your arms, and hope that the instructor can manage the rest. But somehow I didn't much care if I succeeded this time, for I felt I had already accomplished more than I'd hoped to, and was elated. As I swung through the air toward my instructor's outstretched hands, I found myself shouting, "Wooooah! I'm 50!" Then I felt his fingers clasping my wrists, and I was swinging under him in another trapeze. Luckily, I'd had the foresight to bring a digital camera and ask one of my classmates to record the moment. I knew that whatever happened, most of my friends would never believe it. I wanted proof.

Heading back home on the subway, I tried to analyze what all this had meant to me, why I had done it. Was I on some middle-age ego trip? Perhaps. And what if things had turned out less well? What if you've yearned to do something your whole life, then finally try it only to be disappointed? I decided that the important thing was not that I was still agile enough, or insane enough to do this at 50. It was that I still had some dreams left — and the drive to pursue them. It's having that special longing, whatever it may be, that I think we cannot afford to lose — for age is not so much a number as a state of mind. The moment you start feeling that you've done all you wanted, or accomplished all you were meant to, is the moment when you really begin to get old.

The trapeze success made me brave enough to try to satisfy another longing in my 50th year: I started taking tango lessons. My first day, I rode up on the elevator with a man who was undeniably older than I. I could tell he was a student because of the class pass he was holding. But it wasn't his age that caught my attention, it was his schlumpy posture. Like the cocky young trapeze artists, I judged him and made an unkind mental observation about his hopes of being a dancer. His shoulders were hunched, his belly protruding, and when he left the elevator he didn't walk, he waddled. It turned out that he was an advanced student. After our individual classes were over, everyone was invited to partake in an all-school dance party. My schlumpy elevator friend was there, only the moment that a tango started playing, he stood perfectly erect and became almost sensual. Soon every woman in the place was lining up to dance with him. And when he glided with them across the floor, it was as if he had magically morphed into Gene Kelly.

What I learned from this is that no matter our age or appearance, when we're doing something we love, it transforms us. The joy that emanates from within changes how we look — then damn the wrinkles, damn the thinning hair or weakening vision. We radiate. And our age suddenly doesn't matter anymore, because we're fulfilled. ☀

13

Learn to belly dance

Let this beautiful Middle Eastern tradition — sexy, fierce, and energetic — help you fall in love with your 50-year-old body. In this dance, ripeness triumphs over beauty.

BY TaRessa Stovall

A lifelong dance enthusiast, TaRessa Stovall has studied ballet, jazz, tap, and West African dance. She is committed to practicing East African belly dance as an art form, fitness regime, and spiritual journey. She is also coeditor of *Proverbs for the People: Contemporary African-American Literature* (Dafina/Kensington, 2003), co-author of *A Love Supreme: Real-Life Stories of Black Love* (Warner, 2000), and author of *The Buffalo Soldiers* (Chelsea House, 1997).

This dance welcomes you as no other. It does not demand special skills or talent; it does not require experience or reward one body type over another. Women who have excelled at other forms of dance find new challenges in belly dance, while some who have always thought they had two left feet find their natural rhythms, bodysong, and grace.

Young, sleek bodies have no advantage over our riper, more mature bodies. No one measures her neighbor's contours or dress size; there is no reason to compare. This one thing — the bond of womanhood — binds you to the dance and fills you with its possibilities.

"It is a dance of women's power centers — the breasts, the belly, and the hips," says my teacher, Kristen Radden, and all of these things, she emphasizes, are supposed to be full and round! You learn that fleshiness is not bad or revolting or sinful. You come to class and learn to swing what you were taught to suppress and to relax what you've spent your life holding in. You move your body and it moves you and something deep within you shifts, realigns, and is healed.

The music starts and you begin to sway. Slowly at first, then you pick up the rhythm. Each movement is gentle, yet precise. Energetic yet elegant. And ever so fabulously feminine in a very empowering way.

Your lower body is grounded in the energy of the earth. Your middle body mimics the rolling waves of oceans, lakes, and rivers, the dancing flames of fire, and the sensuous swirls of smoke. Your upper body is like pure air — light and graceful as a breeze.

You feel connected to ancient women from around the world — women who danced as part of everyday life, to mark rites of passage, to express emotions that had no words. Women whose movement was prayer, meditation, and spiritual ritual. Your hips move in a circle as you retrace the pathways you have traveled from baby to girl to young woman to adult. From daughter/sister to mother/aunt/godmother/grandmother, from student to professional, from potential to possibility, from purpose to struggle to triumph to promise tested and fulfilled.

You dance to the cycles of your biological imprint: menstruation, pregnancy, birth, and menopause. You dance your biography to music swirling in unfamiliar rhythms, finding freedom in not knowing which way the sound will lead. Something in your body connects to the DNA of your foremothers, and you find yourself performing ancient undulations of the pelvis, mimicking the movements that traditional women worldwide learned in preparation for childbirth.

The music carries you to distant lands as you imagine yourself an innocent womanchild, a sultry temptress, a nurturing lover, a warm mother, a fierce warrior, and an elegant queen just coming into the magic of your personal power.

I am woman! See me flow, see me circle, see me shimmy. I am earth mother, star-child, water maiden, and fire goddess. I am the carrier of life, the nurturer of the world, the beauty of the changing seasons. See my dance — as hopeful as the first sign of spring green; as sensual as the tempting heat of summer; as rich as the falling leaves; as delicate as the unspoiled snow.

You tie on a hip scarf and delight in the swaying of fringe as you learn to shimmy — first slowly, then faster, then in a blur of movement that is almost always accompanied by spontaneous laughter. The little girl — the one who became obscured by the twists, turns, and challenges of growing up and fitting in and meeting expectations and looking, behaving, and moving a certain way — is liberated by the dance. She bursts forth from your heart, where she has been waiting for you to find that "shake it to the East, shake it to the West, shake it to the one that you love the best" beat that frees small girls to dance with innocent abandon.

You find that learning this exotic dance is like learning a new language with an unfamiliar alphabet. As you work to master the basics, you find your mind, body, and spirit striving to unite, for it is in this dance that they will truly work as one. You learn that a dance form that has been misunderstood as sexually bawdy and aggressively brazen in the West is, in fact, subtle, elegant, tender, and sensual in the most delicate and classy way. It makes you feel, simply, lovely.

You are thrilled by the "dress-up" possibilities of the costuming — which is just as addictive as the actual dance! Sumptuous fabrics in riots of color invite you to try on new selves and perhaps discover hidden aspects of yourself in the process. You find yourself mesmerized by the bright jewelry, the alluring makeup — none of which is required, but all of which offers a world of expressive delights. Slipping on sets of finger cymbals gives you access to new rhythms bursting forth from your soul. You are musician and dancer at the same time, moving to a personal interpretation of song.

My fellow dance enthusiasts are doctors, lawyers, accountants, full-time mothers, grandmothers, retirees, college students, military officers, arts administrators, secretaries, and entrepreneurs. None of that matters; once we raise our arms to the music, we are whoever we want to be. We dance with the motion of love discovered, with the sway of a mother comforting a child, with the weight of heartbreak and the fragile promise of love reborn.

Each woman is writing her biography, her truths, her questions and her quests, her sorrows and her triumphs, and the lessons she has learned. In a culture that tells us we are to look like young boys and work like hard-charging men, we relax into the woman-power of softness that embraces and revives us at every level. We eschew our labels, titles, and categories to simply be.

And we shimmy with the sheer, wondrous pleasure of it all. ☀

14

Power up your tennis game

Whether returning to the game or just getting started, tennis at midlife requires a little adjusting.

BY ANGELA BUXTON

Wimbledon champion Angela Buxton made sports history in 1956 when she won the Wimbledon Doubles Championship with partner Althea Gibson. A player and author of books (*Tackle Tennis This Way, Starting Tennis,* and *Winning Tennis and Doubles Tactics*) she has been a professional player, tennis academy owner, coach, and general promoter of the game of tennis in the United States and the United Kingdom. She was a co-founder of The Angela Buxton Tennis Center, one of the most respected International Tennis Academies in the 1970s and 1980s based in Hampstead in London. Over the past thirty years she has been a contributing writer for numerous publications including the *New York Times.* Today she lives in Florida and The United Kingdom and has her own Web site from which this book and others which she has written can be purchased: *www. angelabuxton.com.*

I love tennis, and have been playing it for most of my life. I find the game to be immensely satisfying both physically and intellectually. At its core, it is a thinking game. The appeal for those in their 50s is great: Generally more leisure time becomes available as children go off to school or begin families of their own. Priorities get shifted and staying healthy now gets moved to the top. Tennis is also a great socializer — you'll meet like-minded people.

But if you have played tennis throughout your adult life, you know there are certain inevitable "hiccups." Shots that were once easy to reach may now be harder to get, and your speed on the court may not be what it used to be. Injuries can also be more frequent and more lingering, and it may become harder than ever to recover after a grueling match, especially if you're a weekend tennis warrior.

Here's my to-do list for you:

• *Play less frequently:* If your habit is to play tennis every day, it's a good idea to cut that back to three times a week. Certainly avoid playing two days in a row. By one's 50s, the body really can't take a daily game, and overdoing it can provoke injuries that just may keep you sidelined from any playing at all. What to do between games? Practice your serve — that's always valuable — or consider filling in with another sport that's compatible with tennis, such as swimming or yoga. Because tennis can be stressful on the joints and limbs and swimming and yoga are not, they can help improve the balance in your body. A full body massage is best of all if time and money allow, with particular attention paid to the feet, calves, shoulders, neck, and spine.

• *Stretch:* Certainly by the time you're 50, you should already be doing 10 minutes of stretching before you play, as well as 10 minutes of stretching afterward, as the pros do. Stretch the limbs, knees, quads, Achilles tendons, and calves. Stretch your arms and torso upward (do this against a wall). Reach upward with your left hand as far as you can, and then bending the right arm up your back, clasp your two hands together if you can. Be sure to stretch both sides of the body, too. Tennis can be a one-sided game, and you want to try always to maintain balance.

• *Play with people your own age:* Because physical speed and mental reactions are usually the first things to slow down, don't play with 20- or 30-year-olds. Instead, stay within your own age range (by that I mean play others who are within five years of your own age). One of the biggest problems that over-50 tennis players have is imagining that they're still 20. It may be a bitter pill to swallow, but I have known people who have died on the court and in the locker rooms when they have overexerted themselves.

• *Compensate:* If you've always played singles, consider

putting a time limit on your game (say, a two-hour limit), and eventually, think about playing doubles (there are some experts who will disagree with me here and say that seniors can easily continue to play singles well into their 70s, but I think they're asking for trouble).

If you're a beginner, or even thinking about trying the sport, here's my to-do list for *you:* (Do get a physical first, since tennis is a stressful exercise.)

• *Take it slow:* Don't go from not playing at all to suddenly playing all the time. Take on the game in small doses. Doing too much, too fast can only be discouraging. Remember, you can have a tremendous time at any level of playing. You don't have to be an advanced player or even very good in order to have fun.

• *Take lessons from the start:* In the beginning, it's important to learn the right way to hit the ball and to move on the court, so consider taking lessons from a good professional — about a dozen at minimum. A good instructor can also help you "short-cut" the difficulties, so you'll improve faster than you would on your own. Tip: These days, learning to play tennis is easier than it was 30 years ago, thanks to new methods and different equipment (for example, bigger rackets today have bigger "sweet spots," which make it easier to hit and direct the ball). Before you purchase any equipment, ask your instructor's advice.

• *Stay dry:* Amateur players tend not to realize the consequences of playing a game, then sitting down in a still-damp or wet shirt and having a drink, but professionals know that you must shower and get wet clothes off your body as quickly as possible. When your clothes are damp and sweat dries on your body, it can create stiffness and promote injuries that will hinder your game in the future.

Whether you've been playing tennis all your life or are just starting out, there are certain benefits of tennis that apply to everyone.

One is that by the time you're 50, you tend to play with a bit more equanimity: By that I mean that it's unlikely that you'll get really cross with yourself if you miss a shot; you can laugh if you accidentally flub a long rally or appreciate the game that turns out unexpectedly.

Finally, remember that part of the pleasure and the reward of tennis is the camaraderie — to chat and make new friends with like-minded people who are interested in the same activity as you are. Tennis is a distinctly social sport: You tend to meet people of the same ilk. Especially if you suddenly find yourself on your own for one reason or another, if you can play reasonably well, you may find tennis to be a life-saving social asset, and your phone will ring constantly with invitations to round-robins, games, and the like.

15

Sit still: meditation is medicinal

**Meditation isn't just for the mind and spirit.
It can also benefit your body.**

BY ROBERT H. SCHNEIDER, M.D.

Robert H. Schneider, M.D., has directed about $20 million in funding from the National Institutes of Health for research on transcendental meditation and other aspects of Maharishi Consciousness Based Health Care. He is widely recognized as a leading authority in the area of alternative health, aging, and heart disease. His book *Total Heart Health: Your Complete Program to Prevent and Treat Heart Disease with Maharishi Consciousness Based Health Care,* was published by Basic Health Publications in the fall of 2005. He lives in Fairfield, Iowa.

We used to look forward to birthdays. Our 16th when we could drive; our 18th when we could vote; our 21st, when we graduated from college and truly became adults. Back then, we wanted to see our numbers increase.

But all too soon, increasing numbers were no longer something we looked forward to. Today, it seems, all the numbers are headed in the wrong direction: up. Whether it's our blood pressure, cholesterol, weight, or triglycerides, for most of us, the numbers keep creeping higher as we age.

But I have good news. It's possible to reverse those numbers — without medication! You simply need to sit and meditate for 20 minutes, twice a day.

Yes, sitting quietly for 20 minutes relaxing your mind with transcendental meditation, or TM, the most studied form of meditation, can actually reverse the aging process. Over time, the numbers that determine your physiological age are systematically reduced, even as your chronological age increases. Don't take my word for it; I have the studies to prove it — studies published in some of the top peer-reviewed physiological and medical journals in the world.

First, let's talk about what TM is — and is not.

Let me reassure you that it's not weird or difficult. You don't have to give up steak. You don't have to wear a robe. You don't have to be a New Age hippie. You don't even have to be convinced that it works.

TM technique is surprisingly simple and easy, as natural as falling asleep. In my medical practice and research

I've introduced it to people of all ages from all walks of life. Everyone, regardless of culture, language, gender, ethnicity, philosophy, or religion, has readily taken to this simple practice that makes use of the natural tendency of the mind to settle down and doesn't require concentration or contemplation.

You sit quietly for 20 minutes in the morning and afternoon and use a mantra, or meaningless sound, to let your mind relax. You can do it any place, typically just sitting comfortably in a chair. Whether it's an airport or your living room, you just close your eyes and begin.

The key is to do it in a specific, effortless way. That's why it's necessary to learn the practice from a qualified teacher. Instruction takes about one-and-a-half hours a day for about a week.

What excites me is this: When you sit for 20 minutes, you're not just having a pleasant, relaxing experience. Your brain waves change, your blood chemistry changes, indeed, your whole physiology undergoes changes. Through TM, you have a unique way to gain deep rest in mind and body, which research shows actually stimulates the body's anti-aging repair mechanisms. But stick with TM; studies find it's distinctively effective when compared to other meditation techniques.

As a physician, this thrills me. Too often restoring health means men and women running around in white coats giving shots and pills, cutting people up, shocking their hearts, implanting devices. How wonderful to be able to offer something that isn't harmful or painful, and that can help in so many ways.

Much of our research has been with older folks, who are particularly susceptible to hypertension and heart disease. I love to see how they feel empowered when they learn the TM program. Finally, they're not so dependent on somebody else doing something to them from the outside. They're helping themselves by tapping into their body's inner intelligence so it can heal itself. Often, as their numbers drop, they can even trash their blood pressure medication.

I want to see more of this. I envision a time when people age in a different way from how they do now. In one study, for instance, people who had been practicing TM for more than five years were physiologically 12 years younger than their chronological age, as measured by a drop in blood pressure and improved vision and hearing. Even people who had been practicing TM for just a short time were physiologically five years younger than their chronological age.

Maybe you're asking yourself, "How can this be?" After all, all you're doing is sitting and letting your mind and body settle down. But we find that this pause triggers a host of changes. It's as if your body knows what it wants, and the deep rest for mind and body associated with TM enlivens your body's inner intelligence and gives it a chance to repair the damage associated with daily living.

My collaborators and I have looked at this self-repair mechanism particularly as it relates to cardiovascular disease. After practicing the technique for three months, the people we work with have an average decrease in blood pressure similar to what they'd have if they used medication. When we followed the progress of these older participants for up to 18 years, we found their death rates from heart disease decreased substantially.

What changes are actually going on in the body that lower blood pressure in such magnitude? It turns out that the thickness of the carotid artery, which supplies blood to the head and neck, actually decreased after 12 weeks of TM. This is important because hypertension, or high blood pressure, results in hardening and thickening of the arteries (atherosclerosis), the cause of heart attacks and most strokes. Measuring the thickness of the carotid artery is a good way to measure this change.

Today, thanks in part to our studies, a growing number of medical professionals now recognize the benefits of meditation. Even medical textbooks and medical school classes typically mention its benefits, especially as they relate to heart disease.

The research in other areas is equally fascinating, especially for people in middle age. Studies show, for example, that those who regularly practice TM have greater mental clarity and intelligence. Along with these changes in mind and body come changes in behavior. People who practice TM tend to be more harmonious and happier. And other studies find that the net effect of these changes in mind, body, and behavior can actually make a demonstrable positive change in society. In other words, a healthier, happier you has a positive effect on those around you.

So I suggest that you see turning 50 as an opportunity to take this new direction in revitalizing mind and body — and start reversing those numbers.

Section Four

STAYING STRONG

16

Eat like a caveman

Travel backward in time to recapture the perfect diet. More fruit, less juice; less meat, more nuts.

BY FRED PESCATORE, M.D.

Fred Pescatore, M.D., is the author of a *New York Times* best seller, *The Hamptons Diet*, that weds the health benefits of a Mediterranean-type diet with his strong belief in an optimized balanced nutritional approach. He is also the author of the top-selling books *Thin For Good* and *The Allergy and Asthma Cure*, as well as the top-selling children's health book, *Feed Your Kids Well*.

I bet you're expecting some dull, boring dissertation about eating your spinach and never again spreading butter on your bread. Phooey! If I wrote that, you'd turn the page so fast you might rip it.

Instead, I've got another option for you when it comes to eating right (and losing weight without trying): Eat like a cave dweller.

Yup, you heard me right. If we all ate the way we're genetically programmed to — the way our great-great-great-great (etc., etc.) grandparents ate and lived, there'd be no need for diets, weight-loss pills, or low-fat ice cream.

Just imagine what your ancestors' diet must have been like; they ate only foods they could catch, pick, or steal from other tribes. Aside from the threat of death from a rampaging mammoth, you can't get much healthier than that. This feast-or-famine lifestyle was imbedded in their genes; they hung onto every calorie they could find because they never knew where the next meal was coming from. Unfortunately, they've passed that "thrifty gene" down to us, even though we live in a culture where there's food everywhere we turn. So we continue to store fat for that day when we can't find any food. The best way around this? Eat like our ancestors did. This means:

1. *Keep away from fast foods.* That's right. Put the burger down and slowly step away. Although you know this, how many of you still ate at a McDonald's this week? Even the healthier options in the drive-thru are nutritionally suspect. Some of the salads have more fat and calories than the burgers.

2. *Eat lean proteins.* Your cave grandparents would be able to catch only wild animals, which are leaner than

the meats we eat today. So stick with white meat chicken or turkey, pork, and fish, and trim the fat from all red meats. Even better: Try some game animals yourself. Buffalo, bison, elk, venison — they're all lower in fat than the sirloin you might have had last night.

3. *Load up on fruits and vegetables.* Your cave relatives ate whatever grew in the ground or on trees, so the more of these you get, the better. Although today's dietary guidelines call for nine servings a day, research shows that upping the amount you eat by just one or two servings a day can significantly reduce your risk for disease. Potatoes, peas, corn, and other starchy vegetables don't count. Instead, make healthier choices like asparagus, broccoli, kale, spinach, and other dark leafy greens. As for fruits, choose those with the least amount of sugar, such as berries and melons, and try to avoid tropical fruits such as bananas (which contain 66 grams of sugar on average), mangoes, and pineapple.

4. *Stick to whole grains.* We've been eating these for 10,000 years. Then, about 100 years ago, refined grains (with all the fiber and nutrients stripped away) came into vogue. During the past 20 years, consumption of refined grains has skyrocketed and, not coincidentally, so have rates of obesity. So stick to fiber- and nutrient-filled brown rice and whole-grain breads and pasta.

Make sure you read the labels: Look for the word "whole" in the ingredient list.

5. *Munch on nuts and seeds.* Nuts contain heart-healthy Omega-3 fatty acids, and studies show that the more you eat, the lower your risk for heart disease. Plus, snacking on nuts can even help you lose weight. That's not permission to go crazy on the cashews, however. Stick to one ounce a day (about a handful) if you're trying to lose weight and two ounces a day otherwise. Also, choose healthy versions such as almonds, walnuts, and macadamias.

6. *Avoid fruit juice.* Cave dwellers certainly didn't pluck a carton of orange juice off a tree; they ate an orange! Overall, fruit juice is only slightly healthier for you than soda and often has more calories. Studies find that the more fruit juice you drink, the fatter you're likely to be and the more likely you are to develop diabetes.

7. *Pick the right fats.* Although there are many oils available, science points toward monounsaturated fats as the healthiest ones. That means olive and macadamia nut oil, with its high smoke point, for high-heat cooking. You also want to avoid trans fats, found in most processed foods. As little as three grams a day can significantly increase your risk for heart disease and stroke (an average donut has nine grams of trans fat). Read ingredient lists: Avoid "partially hydrogenated" anything.

8. *Choose local and seasonal foods.* Isn't it kind of weird to be eating peaches in January? Not only is it more expensive, but scientists are beginning to find that our bodies are best at absorbing nutrients locally grown, in season.

9. *Go organic whenever possible.* Sure, organic foods might cost a bit more and be harder to find, but they're worth it. They're not inundated with chemicals, and they contain trace mineral and natural antioxidants often missing in conventionally grown produce. Plus, the more organic foods we buy, the higher the demand will be, and the lower the price.

10. *Learn to cook.* It's not that hard. Spend a weekend cooking for the week ahead and all you have to do is reheat something at night. To that end, make sure you also invest in the proper kitchen gadgets. Start with a good knife, a slow cooker (place everything you want to eat for dinner in the pot, go to work, and come home to a delicious meal), and an herb grinder.

Follow these few "rules" and you'll be eating like the cave dwellers in no time at all — and in the end, you'll be healthier, thinner, and less prone to disease. After all, you've still got most of your life ahead of you — live it to the fullest! ☀

17

Take heart

While the rules for heart-health are different for men and women, there are rules. And they can save you from heart disease.

BY DAVID KATZ, M.D.

David Katz, M.D., is the director of medical studies in public health and a lecturer in medicine at Yale University School of Medicine. He also cofounded and directs the school's Prevention Research Center, a clinical research facility funded by the Centers for Disease Control that is devoted to chronic disease prevention. Katz, who lives in Derby, Connecticut, is a nutrition columnist for *O: the Oprah Magazine*, and also writes a weekly column syndicated through *The New York Times*.

Perhaps men truly are from Mars and women from Venus. Certainly there are more than enough times when it feels as if we belong on separate planets. But while a woman's heart and a man's heart may beat to the tune of different drummers, both are sustained by the same vulnerable blood supply. If you

104

subject yourself to stress, tobacco smoke, a sedentary lifestyle, poor nutrition, and/or obesity, you succumb quite comparably to heart disease whether you're a man or a woman.

Heart disease is the leading killer of men and women in the United States. In fact, heart disease kills more than 10 times as many women as breast cancer; more women die every year from heart disease than from all cancers put together, making it as much a woman's disease as a man's.

But enough lamenting: Exercise your power! Heart disease is eminently preventable. I want you to acknowledge your vulnerabilities not so you succumb to them, but so you recognize, confront, and conquer them. *Veni, vidi, vici,* and all that. You've come, you've seen, so let's conquer.

Heart disease is due to the accumulation of plaque, or "atherogenesis," in the coronary arteries, which can be caused by almost anything that damages blood vessel linings. It takes plaque years to accumulate to a dangerous degree, which is why our hearts may break in our youth, but they rarely fail until we are a bit more, shall we say, mature.

That's not to say, however, that there aren't danger signs along the way. We call these "signs of cardiac risk." And while it would be great to have a single test that could tell you whether or not your risk for heart disease is elevated, we're just not there yet. Instead, we've got an array of important measures.

Let's start with blood pressure. High blood pressure can directly injure blood vessels by striking the inner lining with excessive force over and over again. You can just imagine the damage that causes! Ideally, your blood pressure should be below 120/80. And while there are numerous effective medications that can lower blood pressure if and when bona fide "hypertension" or high blood pressure develops, don't wait to find yourself on the wrong side of that line.

Lower your blood pressure and your risk of hypertension through physical activity, maintaining a healthy weight, and limiting the amount of salt in your diet.

Perhaps the best-known cardiac risk factor you can change is your cholesterol level. You know about cholesterol, right? It's a blood fat that travels throughout your blood and can build up in your arteries. Cholesterol is no longer a simple, single measurement, but is derived from several measures that comprise your "lipid panel." You want your LDL (that's the bad stuff), triglycerides, and total cholesterol to be relatively low, and your HDL (that's the good stuff) to be relatively high to minimize your heart disease risk.

The best way to get there? Eat only small amounts of saturated fat (found in red meat and full-fat dairy products) and trans fats (found in processed foods and often identified as "partially hydrogenated oil") while getting plenty of soluble fiber from oats, barley, beans, lentils, and fruit. And make sure you're pursuing regular physical activity and working to maintain a healthy weight. Raising a glass can raise HDL, too; one alcoholic drink per day for women and up to two per day for men can be very good for your heart.

Oxidation can injure blood vessels and change cholesterol particles in ways that make it easier for them to gunk up your arteries. The real bad actor in atherogenesis is "oxidized LDL," a form of super bad cholesterol. You can minimize this form by filling your diet with antioxidants. It's not hard: Just focus on vegetables, fruits, red wine, tea, and — you heard me right — *dark chocolate.*

Of course, there's more to a heart attack than just an accumulation of plaque. The plaque itself has to be soft enough to rupture. And blood platelets, special blood cells that help blood clot, need to be sticky enough to pile up at the rupture site and block the flow of blood through the damaged area. Once that blood flow with its life-carrying oxygen stops, you've got yourself a heart attack.

So the consistency of your plaque and the stickiness of your platelets are other signs of heart disease risk we can both measure and change. For instance, inflammation (the process that occurs when you injure yourself) tends to make plaque soft and vulnerable. One way to reduce inflammation is to eat fish, such as salmon, regularly. An even better bet is to take a daily fish oil supplement. Fish oil can also help make your platelets less sticky, as can vitamin E.

While there are many ways to measure cardiac risks, a few simple strategies serve to improve those risks:

Don't smoke.

Engage in regular physical activity, accumulating at least 30 minutes of moderate exertion (i.e., you can still talk while you're exercising, but you probably can't sing) each day if possible.

Eat a balanced diet, rich in vegetables, fruits, and whole grains.

Control your weight.

Limit your intake of processed foods.

Control the stress in your life if possible, or at least your responses to it: Try yoga or meditation.

Take a multivitamin and a fish oil supplement. (B vitamins help maintain and repair healthy tissues. If in doubt about which vitamin to choose, sign on to www.consumerlab.com for an objective appraisal of the choices. I also recommend up to 200 IU of vitamin E per day, but no more; if you're taking a good daily multivitamin, you're likely getting enough.)

If you've done all this and you still have risk factors indicating a high risk of heart disease, that's the time to turn to medicine — but not before.

And remember: There are — or at least have been — entire cultures in which heart disease is virtually unknown. Not because the people don't have a genetic predisposition for heart disease, but because of their healthy habits. You can virtually eliminate your heart disease risk. The very heart of self-defense is in your hands. ☀

18

Bone up

Be good to your joints and bones now. Be limber later.

BY MICHAEL R. WILSON, M.D.

Michael Wilson, M.D., is a board-certified orthopaedic surgeon with more than 25 years of experience who sees thousands of patients each year for ailments that range from arthritis to sports-related injuries. He practices at the Ochsner Clinic Foundation in New Orleans and is also an assistant clinical professor of surgery at both Tulane University Medical School and the Uniformed Services University of Health Sciences.

OK, let's get one thing straight: You don't just wake up at age 50 and suddenly notice those aches and pains. They've been creeping up on you, right? The question now is, what can you do about them today and what can you do to improve the likelihood that you won't be limping into the future?

First, it's important to understand that there are two separate issues here. One is the health of your joints; the other is the health of your bones. It's easy to get the two confused. Even the terms we use for the illness of each — osteoarthritis for worn-out joints and osteoporosis for thinning of the bones — sound alike.

So let's start with osteoarthritis, since I've probably spent more time in my career explaining what it is and isn't than in any other conversation with a patient. Americans seem to think that arthritis is some sort of minor problem that, although irritating, should go away with Tylenol or Advil. In fact, osteoarthritis is a chronic, progressive, often crippling condition. It is the main reason orthopedic surgeons like myself perform more than half a million total hip and knee replacements in this country every year.

Yet patients are often shocked and even disappointed to find out that what's wrong with them is "just arthritis." "I'm in such pain!" they wail. "Don't try to tell me that it is just arthritis!"

Well, just arthritis is enough to force you to use a cane or crutches, keep you from sleeping, or steal your ability to walk from point A to point B. When it affects your hands, it can make the simplest activity either miserably painful or downright impossible. I see 50-year-old women who can't open a pill bottle and guys my age (54) who can't button a shirt. The preference of osteoarthritis for the spine, particularly the lower back, is one of the universal miseries of mankind and the most common reason Americans miss work or become permanently disabled.

I find it useful to understand end-stage osteoarthritis as organ failure in which the organ that fails is the joint. When your kidneys fail, you might go on dialysis. Eventually, if you're lucky, you get a kidney transplant. When your knee fails, it might be a slower process but in the end it can lead to total knee replacement — the orthopedic equivalent of a kidney transplant.

Osteoarthritis can result from damage, injury, or even inherited weakness in any of the structural components that work together to create a healthy joint. It is not just one disease but the common final outcome that results from many insults to the joint.

The big three symptoms of osteoarthritis are pain, swelling, and stiffness, in any combination and with any degree of severity. It's fairly easy to diagnose with a physical examination and x-rays.

If you're like most 50-year-olds, you're ready at this point for the cure. Bad news — osteoarthritis can't be cured. So early on, the goal is to control your symptoms through exercise, simple medicines like acetaminophen (Tylenol), nonsteroidal anti-inflammatory drugs (NSAIDS) like ibuprofen or naproxen, and the so-called "chondro-protective" (literally, "cartilage protecting") agents like glucosamine and chondroitin. (They help some patients and have no effect on others. Try a preparation that includes both for at least six weeks. If you feel better, keep taking it. If you don't, you're wasting your money.) As the disease progresses, these approaches may become less effective. Then, more aggressive surgical management, including joint replacement, may be necessary.

Notice I haven't said anything about diet. The only thing to know about diet and arthritis is that you should watch your weight: Our joints are simply not designed to effectively support more than our ideal body weight.

If you do get to the point where you need a hip, knee, or shoulder replaced, you are looking at one of the most successful operations in the history of surgery — 90 to 95 percent of all patients who have these surgeries end up with a good or excellent result.

Now let's talk about thinning of the bones, or osteoporosis. Although this applies to women more than men, don't quit reading here, guys. Osteoporosis in men is doubly stealthy. It's overlooked in men just as it is in women because there are no symptoms at first; and it's ignored because we think of osteoporosis as almost purely a disease of women. Yet men have a greater risk of developing osteoporosis than prostate cancer!

Here's what's happening. We build up a certain amount of bone in our bone mineral bank by age 20 or so and then we either maintain it or spend it. We make deposits in the bone mineral bank by maintaining a dietary calcium intake of greater than 1,500 mg a day and a vitamin D intake of 400 to 800 IU per day, and by performing weight-bearing exercises such as walking, aerobics, tennis, or weight lifting. It's hard to get enough calcium in your diet to meet that requirement, however. So plan on taking a daily calcium supplement.

We make withdrawals via drinking diet soda, turning into a couch potato, smoking, drinking alcohol, and, if you're a woman, childbirth, breastfeeding, and the loss of estrogen that occurs with menopause.

The stakes are high. Osteoporosis leads to fractures — broken hips, compression fractures of the vertebrae, broken wrists and ankles. One in four women age 45 already has measurable osteoporosis, as do nine of 10 women over age 75. There are now more than 300,000 hip fractures per year in the United States. As our Baby Boomer generation ages (that would be you), researchers estimate this figure will double by 2015. Here's how to keep from being part of that statistic.

The gold standard to measure the strength of your bones, or bone mineral density (BMD), is the "DEXA" (dual electron x-ray absorptiometry) scan. Since it's not considered routine, don't be afraid to press your doctor for this. Treatment includes calcium, vitamin D, and one or more of the newer drugs that actually can restore bone density. Over time, these drugs may actually increase your bone mineral density, decreasing the rate and severity of fractures. (Women can also discuss the value of estrogen supplementation with their doctors.)

At 50, you need to know where you stand: Exercising regularly, keeping your weight down, watching what you eat, and avoiding injury will help keep both bones and joints strong.

19

Buff up your brain

No more jokes about "senior moments." Keeping your brain at its highest level is easier than you think.

BY BILL E. BECKWITH, PH.D.

As the founder of Life and Memory Center in Naples, Florida, Dr. Beckwith has helped thousands of baby boomers and seniors "work out" their brain to keep it in peak condition. With over 30 years of experience, he specializes in the four pillars of successful aging: finance, health, memory and happiness. He received his degrees from Ohio State University and taught at the University of North Dakota. He also established the Center for Excellence in Memory Care and served as clinical director of a major memory disorders clinic.

As I look into the mirror each morning, I know that I've changed. I don't look like I did when I was 30. The changes are obvious: My hair is gray, I have more wrinkles, and my skin has markings and blemishes it didn't have in my younger days. I don't always like these changes, but at least I can see them.

What are not so obvious are the changes that occur inside. For instance, I know that my bones aren't as dense as they once were; that my muscle strength and endurance have declined. I'm lucky; living a healthy life-style has helped keep these changes fairly minimal, and they haven't caused any significant disability.

But what about my brain? Yup, your brain also changes as you age. Rather than weakening, like your muscles, it shrinks. In fact, your brain's potential peaks at age two, when it contains the largest number of cells it will ever have. It's all downhill from there!

That doesn't mean your brain *function* has to go down-hill. We've learned a lot about what constitutes memory, what affects it, and what can be done to maintain it. Like an athlete who has to work out every day to stay in shape, you have to exercise your brain to maintain its health. But maintaining your memory goes beyond your brain; today we know that anything that affects the health of your body also affects the health of your brain. That means if you have high cholesterol, are overweight, smoke, have diabetes, eat an unhealthy diet, or don't get enough physical exercise your brain will suffer.

Suffer how? Well, by experiencing more of those memory blips that come as you age. You can't think of a word when you want; you have problems multitasking; you find yourself making inadvertent word substitutions, forgetting names, misplacing items. I'm not talking Alzheimer's disease here; I'm talking age-related memory loss.

And no, just because you may have already noticed some of these symptoms, it's never too late to slow the cycle. Another thing we've learned in recent years is that the brain is remarkably pliable, able to create new connections and new neural pathways to compensate for those that might have already been lost.

Start by stimulating your mind with mental exercise. Look at what you're currently doing for mental stimulation. If it's watching reality shows and reading *People* magazine, you're in trouble. You need to stretch your brain, continue learning, expose yourself to new experiences. These can be as minor as taking a new route to work every day and as major as returning to school for another degree. As simple as completing the daily crossword puzzle and as complex as learning a new language. How about a new hobby, like growing orchids, or collecting wine? (New evidence showing moderate alcohol use can improve memory provides an additional incentive.)

Now take a look at your exercise program. Do you do some form of aerobic exercise for 40 minutes most days of the week? Do you have a resistance training routine? Both forms of exercise appear to contribute uniquely to mental efficiency. They also help your memory by helping you manage stress.

At the same time, you need to pay attention to what you're eating. Thanks to research over the past 20 years, we now know what kind of diet helps maintain a strong mind. That would be lots of fruits and vegetables. A minimum of saturated fats and salt. Regular servings of fish instead of red meat. And don't forget that glass of red wine.

Now, what if you've already noticed some of those age-related memory lapses? No problem, just follow a few clever tricks to help you over the rough spots. For example, learn how to use your calendar, *really* use your calendar. Too often, the only things on our calendar are those things we *have* to do. How about adding things we'd *like* to do, or simply need to remember? For instance, schedule in those 40 minutes of exercise each day. Schedule surprises for your spouse, like sending flowers or a card, calls to your mother, reminders to get the furnace checked, clean the filters, water the plants. There's no reason you have to carry the minutia of everyday life around in your head; write it down!

Another external memory aid is to add things you need to remember to your daily routine. For instance, how do you remember to take your blood pressure medication (or multivitamin) consistently? Put the pill bottle in front of your toothbrush. Then it becomes part of an already-ingrained habit (I hope that brushing your teeth is a daily habit!).

Worried you'll forget important points of a conversation? Carry a small tape recorder with you to record these discussions (with the other person's OK, of course) so you can review them later and have a chance to reflect on them. For example, taking your tape recorder to physician visits will help you remember complicated information and medical directions (plus, your attorney will love it).

Always forgetting where your keys and wallet are? Create a take-away spot. Each evening, put the things you need for the following day next to the garage door (or whatever door you use to leave your house). Have a place for everything and put everything in its place. For instance, when you take off your glasses, always put them in the assigned spot, no matter how inconvenient, now matter how tired you are. I guarantee you won't forget where they are.

Right about now, you're thinking: He hasn't told me anything I don't already know. Of course! A healthy mind is all a matter of common sense. Follow these simple tips and you'll find that aging is not a disease to be avoided, but a journey of personal growth. With these steps, you can travel to the end of the journey with your memory and mind intact. ☀

20

Stop squinting

**There are safe and simple ways to ward off bifocals
and help you see your future clearly.**

BY BRIAN S. BOXER WACHLER, M.D.

Brian S. Boxer Wachler, M.D., is the founding director of the
Boxer Wachler Vision Institute in Beverly Hills, California.
The former director of the UCLA Laser Refractive Center
at the Jules Stein Eye Institute in Los Angeles, he has
pioneered surgical techniques and guidelines that have
become the industry standard. He also serves as an investi-
gator for numerous FDA clinical trials.

How do you know you're turning 50? When a friend
or spouse says to you with a little grin, "This is a
big birthday for you . . . let's have a party with all
your friends," then hands you an invitation you can't
read because you left your reading glasses at the office.
Losing your ability to read anything, anywhere, without special equipment can be as mortifying as knowing
that the AARP membership application is just around
the corner.

This decline in your reading vision is called presbyopia, which means "aging eyes." It's an awful name, isn't it? So, if you don't mind, I've come up with my own translation: maturing eyes, which lends a certain grace to the process. After all, just think how much better it would have sounded if, when you first began having trouble seeing up close in your 40s, your eye doctor told you, "No need to worry, you've got the condition known as 'maturing eyes,' that's all." Somehow, that might have lessened the blow. In fact, you might have looked in the mirror and enthusiastically said to yourself, "I really do look more mature!"

While maturing eyes are largely unavoidable, you can take comfort in numbers. It's been a human condition ever since we made it past age 40 thousands of years ago. Of course, some greats in history were able to bypass the maturing eyes condition. Take Wolfgang Amadeus Mozart. He avoided maturing eyes not because his musical genius flowed over into his eyesight, but because he died at the age of 34 (before presbyopia hit).

So, when you consider the alternative, a few pairs of reading glasses don't seem like a huge price to pay for good sight.

In the past, that was the only option people with presbyopia had. Incredibly organized people stashed pairs all over their house, office, car, etc., buying them in bulk like diapers. Some tried to make the best of the situation with designer frames, refusing to be caught with a "granny glasses chain" around the neck. But there was no hiding it: They were still wearing reading glasses.

Today, however, those of us of a certain age are in luck: We have other options that may decrease our need for reading glasses. For instance, today there are bifocal contact lenses especially for reading vision.

If you're willing to go the surgical route, there are also minimally invasive vision correction procedures like LASIK, LTK, and CK that can help with presbyopia. You're probably familiar with at least the first in that alphabet soup of laser surgeries: LASIK. In this procedure, a tiny flap is created in the cornea (the outer windshield part of the eye) and a laser is used to reshape the eye to focus your vision. LASIK for reading vision is most often used when your distance vision has also declined.

In LTK and CK, the doctor uses either laser energy (LTK) or radiofrequency energy (CK) to heat spots on your cornea to refocus your vision. Each is best for patients who still have very good distance vision, but for whom close vision, i.e., reading, is the only problem.

Not everyone will be a good candidate for reading vision contact lenses, LASIK, LTK, or CK. Ask your eye doctor to evaluate you and discuss these options.

But have realistic expectations. Even though these techniques can significantly reduce your need for reading glasses, there is still no "silver bullet" that will give you perfect vision all the time without occasionally whipping out those extra spectacles.

That may change in the future, however. Researchers, including myself, are working on some exciting new procedures, such as implants placed inside the eye that allow your reading muscles to work again, which may vanquish the need for reading glasses forever.

Symptoms of maturing eyes do not stop with affected reading vision. Also watch out for "dry eye syndrome," a burning, aching, gritty feeling in your eyes. It can hit first thing in the morning, leaving you with red eyes for the rest of the day or, if you wear contact lenses, force you to switch over to glasses.

The good news is that dry eyes can be treated with over-the-counter artificial tear drops. Also, swallowing a teaspoon of flaxseed oil or three flaxseed oil capsules a day can work wonders, not only for your eyes, but for your dry skin, too! Nonetheless, see your eye doctor to make sure nothing more serious is going on.

In fact, that's about the best advice I can give you as you hit the half-century mark: See your eye doctor, whether ophthalmologist or optometrist, for a thorough eye exam every year. Be sure your doctor checks for "quiet" diseases that might be brewing such as glaucoma, cataracts, and early signs of macular degeneration. This is also a good time to discuss options to make your mature eyes less "mature." Then, maybe, by the time your next big birthday rolls around, those reading glasses will be a distant memory.

21

Stop the flash: eat soy and flax

Sometimes, women can manage those "power surges" with a simple change in diet.

BY DOROTHY FOLTZ-GRAY

Dorothy Foltz-Gray has been a freelance writer and editor specializing in health, fitness, food, and personal essays for 17 years. She is the author of *Make Pain Disappear* (Reader's Digest Health Publishing), a co-author of *Food Cures* (Reader's Digest Health Publishing, 2007), and author of *Alternative Treatments for Arthritis: An A to Z Guide* (Arthritis Foundation, 2005). A contributing editor for *Health Magazine*, her work has appeared in *Bon Appetit; Cooking Light; Good Housekeeping; Ladies Home Journal; Parenting; Prevention; O, The Oprah Magazine; Reader's Digest; Redbook; Real Simple; Spry; Woman's Day;* and others. She is also an editor and writer for *Lifescript.com.*

L ooking for an alternative to reduce menopausal symptoms and benefit your hormonal health? For many women at age 50-plus, the answer may lie in a combination of soy and flaxseed. This dynamic duo can be found in a multitude of natural foods from granola to chips to waffles.

Sales of soy foods have increased 44 percent since 2001, and flax has become known as the richest vegetarian source of Omega-3 essential fatty acids, prompting even mainstream bakers to sell flaxseed-enriched breads. But what explains the sudden urge to combine these two in so many products?

The answer is that both soy and flaxseed contain phytoestrogens (plant estrogens), which can mimic human estrogen, and for the 50-something woman, they can be an alternative to HRT (hormone replacement therapy). In fact, there has been a lot of talk that soy and flax can help relieve menopausal symptoms, like hot flashes. Since soy and flaxseed are cousins but not identical twins — the phytoestrogens in flaxseed, called lignans, have a significantly different structure from the soy phytoestrogens — they may work differently in the body. Combining soy and flax in foods like protein bars and waffles may offer two sources of health protection; however, there's no hard evidence yet to suggest that their combined effect is greater than that of each alone.

Of course, just about the time that women 50 and over were hearing the great news about soy, research was showing that slurping down vast quantities of soymilk or soybean chili might actually increase your risk of breast cancer. As so often happens with modern medical dilemmas, newspaper headlines fluctuated back and forth, one week trumpeting the benefits of taking in ample amounts of phytoestrogens, and the next week decrying the risks. It's tricky to figure out whether to stock up on soy-and-flaxseed cereal or avoid the aisles brimming with snacks touting the duo. Will the pair tame your hot flashes and restless sleep? Will they lower your breast cancer risk or bump it up?

The truth is that both flaxseed and soy reduce menopausal symptoms, a boon to any 50-plus woman who's spent even one night thrashing through night sweats (the closest experience to life as a strobe light). Studies show that just one serving of soy each day (a half-cup of tofu) reduces hot flashes by 10 to 20 percent (HRT reduces hot flashes by 60 percent). Such studies have led both the American Menopause Foundation and the North American Menopause Society to recommend soy.

And in 30 studies, soy didn't raise estrogen levels. Theoretically that's a good thing, since increased estrogen may stimulate tumor growth, increasing the risk of breast cancer. Soy may also increase the length of the menstrual cycle by one day, which is also a good thing, since longer cycles are associated with decreased risk of breast cancer. And flaxseed may block prostaglandins, hormone-like substances that, when released in excess during menstruation, can cause heavy bleeding.

Meanwhile, the jury is still out on the effect of soy protein and phytoestrogens on bone density. Some studies show that for postmenopausal women, eating soy slightly reduces bone loss; others show it brings about no improvement.

The flaxseed story is simpler: Some research shows that flaxseed reduces the risk of breast cancer and slows tumor growth. But the central gift of flaxseed is the heart-healthy Omega-3 fatty acids that help lower cholesterol and reduce clogging in the arteries. In 50-something men, those acids may also help fight inflammation in the prostate gland, keep sperm healthy, and improve penile blood flow, which in turn checks impotence. And the body simply needs those fatty acids — often difficult for vegetarians to come by — to help cell membranes take in nutrients better while barring harm.

Experts recommend eating about one-quarter cup of ground flaxseed (whole flax seeds aren't generally digested), or one to three tablespoons of flaxseed oil each day. If you haven't succumbed to one of those soy-and-flax products, you may want to sprinkle ground flaxseed on yogurt, cereal, soup, or salads.

Despite the ever-changing news stories, the best evidence suggests that when you grab a flax-and-soy snack, you're benefiting your 50-something hormonal health — or at least doing it no harm. Soy is a terrific low-fat protein and both it and flaxseed are great for your heart and your cholesterol levels. So don't skimp on this dynamic duo.

22

Look within: get a colonoscopy

Okay, it's nasty. But all you need to get through this life-saving rite of passage is a sense of humor.

BY PATRICIA L. RAYMOND, M.D.

Patricia Raymond, M.D., founder of Rx For Sanity (RxForSanity.com), is the author of the colonoscopy joke anthology *Colonoscopy: It'll Crack U Up!* and is a frequent contributor to and editorial board member of *Family Doctor: The Magazine That Makes Housecalls.* Board certified in gastroenterology and a fellow of both the American Colleges of Physicians and the American College of gastro-enterology, she practices in Chesapeake, Virginia.

I figured out early on that the only way to get the horrified look off people's faces when I told them what I do for a living (I'm a gastroenterologist) was to learn to poke fun at what I do and who I am. So I frequently introduce myself as a "butt meddler" or a "big buttinski." Which is why I feel qualified and, indeed, allowed, to give you a particularly personal, some might even say intimate, message as you enter your 50th year: Get a colonoscopy now!

You think I'm going to harp on the medical reasons for colonoscopy, don't you? About how 40 percent of 40-year-olds have one or more polyps — little fleshy mushroom-like growths — sprouting in their colon. About how, over a 10- to 12-year span, these polyps turn into cancer in about six out of 100 people. About how, as the second-leading cause of cancer death, colon cancer is not to be taken lightly. And about how, given all these reasons, you need a colonoscopy now to look for and remove those polyps.

Naaahhhh. Too easy. Instead, I'm going to tweak two of your darkest desires: greed and the quest for fame.

"Greed?" you echo excitedly, spittle forming at the corners of your mouth. "A colonoscopy can make me rich?"

Sure. Just consider the late great Italian artist Piero Manzoni. If you didn't have your finger on the pulse of the 1960s pop art movement, you might not be familiar with Signor Manzoni's BM art. In 1961, he canned his solid excretory material in some 90 tins. These exclusive exhibits were sold to art collectors when they were hot (pun intended) at peak poop prices as high as $75,000.

Even today, prices remain steep for a Manzoni tin; in June 2002, the respected Tate Gallery in London purchased tin No. 04 for about $38,000. Beyond the artistic value of the tins, however, there's another reason for the high prices: They're becoming increasingly rare. Seems that as time passes, half of the canned art has exploded.

Given that you can expect to expel about seven pounds of "debris" during your pre-colonoscopy cleansing prep, with careful collection and skillful marketing you, too, could hit the mother lode. An added bonus: transient weight loss. You may be able to fit into those "thin" jeans in the back of your closet!

Now, about that shot at fame (and I'm not just talking about the glare of our internal spotlight on your colon). While our generation is enthralled with buttocks (from the rounded slopes of J-Lo to *South Park*'s Cartman and his adventures with the alien anal probe), our modern stars are nothing compared to the artistry of the great Petomaine, a Frenchman who was a sensation in Western Europe in the late 1800s.

A headline performer at the famed Moulin Rouge, Petomaine was known for his anal imitations and his ability to play wind instruments with his rectal control. Yes, this fartist was also a flautist. His legacy has not faded into oblivion. Now on the scene one may find an English former train conductor, stage name Mr. Methane, making a tidy living with what he calls "Controlled Anal Voicing."

What does this have to do with a colonoscopy, you ask. Well, any gastroenterologist will be happy to provide you with an opportunity to entertain the post-op crowd with controlled anal voicing as you expel the gas after your colonoscopy.

In all seriousness, however (and I take colon cancer very seriously), a colonoscopy is not nearly as nasty as it sounds. Here's how it works: First we flush you out, a universally disliked bit of extreme house-cleaning. Then, after you check in and receive your IV and some really great drugs, we skillfully advance a flexible lighted endoscope around your colon (where, regardless of what your spouse or coworkers say, we rarely find your head).

We then inflate your colon with air to inspect the lining. If we find polyps, we snip them on our way out . . . as simple as that. The part with the hose only takes about 20 minutes — the whole shebang with check-in and recovery about two hours. If we don't find any polyps, we'll stop nagging you for 10 years; if we remove a polyp or you have a close relative with colon cancer, we'll see you back for a repeat personal periscopic party in five years.

The key is having fun while you're doing it. For instance, I encourage my patients to decorate their bottoms to celebrate various holidays that fall on or near their scheduled colonoscopy. Over the years, I've been greeted with hearts, pumpkins and black cats, even an American flag or two. Just imagine my surprise when I pulled back the sheet covering an elderly woman on Abraham Lincoln's birthday and found a miniaturized version (oh, the wonders of computers) of the Gettysburg Address taped to one lower cheek.

What can be done "by the people and for the people" if you do have a polyp? Don't panic. First, wait for the pathology report on your polyp. Many polyps are benign, meaning they're not ever going to turn cancerous. If you do grow the premalignant kind (called "adenomas"), a healthy diet full of fruits and vegetables and low in animal fat, vigorous exercise, high calcium intake, and a daily baby aspirin — all the things you know you should be doing anyway — will reduce your odds of growing more.

So get off your butt and get your colonoscopy scheduled today!

Section Five

MANAGING YOUR
CAREER AT MIDLIFE

Reappraise yourself

In your 50s, you're more valuable to your employer than you realize. But it's up to you to show the boss what you're worth.

BY MARY FURLONG

President and founder of Mary Furlong & Associates, Mary has spent the last 20 years guiding the digital marketing strategies of major U.S. Corporations for their 45-plus age markets. She served as an adviser to the president and Congress during the Clinton Administration and is executive professor of Entrepreneurship and Women in Leadership at Santa Clara University, Leavy School of Business, in Silicon Valley. Mary Furlong has appeared on CBS, *The Today Show*, PBS, and NPR to discuss issues related to trends in aging and technology. *Time* Magazine recognized her contribution as chairman of ThirdAge Media by honoring her in 1999 as one of its "Digital 50."

There is an old joke that says the closest most people come to perfection is on an employment application. Even if that's true, career professionals just turning 50 might be the next best example of perfection, at least when it comes to job productivity.

How's that, you say? How can a 50-year-old bring more to the table than an up-and-coming 25-year-old or seasoned-and-savvy 37-year-old just hitting his or her stride?

I think it's a no-brainer. Older workers bring a plethora of benefits to the workplace. They have more intellectual knowledge, having spent more years honing their craft and getting to know their industry and their company.

How about leadership and, by extension, mentorship? More-experienced workers often set the tone for professionalism in the workplace. They've seen it all, faced just about every challenge, and are rarely surprised by events, either good or bad. There is a lot to be said for a steady, calm hand on the corporate steering wheel in times of crisis. Fifty-something workers possess such attributes in spades.

Unfortunately, older workers still face something of a stigma in the workplace and in their careers. "The end is in sight," critics say. "He/she is a great worker and valuable contributor, but might be getting a bit long in the tooth. Maybe we should bring in someone younger . . . and cheaper."

Okay, you won't find any management types uttering those words publicly, but you just know that the sentiment is out there. Out with the old and in with the new, and all that.

How can 50-somethings fight back against this "soft" bias against older workers? Simple. By showing management that you still possess a great deal of value, and indeed, are irreplaceable.

What makes a 50-something an irreplaceable worker? I maintain that it's a combination of the attributes of attitude, ambition, enthusiasm, integrity, determination, discipline, and work ethic to become a lean, mean, career-advancing machine — even at age 50. These workers still contribute across the board and are not easily pigeonholed by age, gender, ethnicity, or any other demographic a pointy-headed academic can roll out. What makes them stand out in a crowd is their record of achievement, as well as the smiles on their faces — they're doing what they love to do.

"Hey," you might say, reading this. "I have all those attributes, but nobody's calling me irreplaceable." But success is more than simply having the tools to succeed. Irreplaceable professionals are those who take these attributes and use them creatively. Here are some examples:

Irreplaceable 50-something career professionals . . .

. . . Still actively seek to get ahead.
Invariably, these workers ask, "How can I make a larger contribution?" It's contributions that make successful

careers, especially in the long run. Successful 50-something professionals are never passive. That's why they are promoted, and then promoted again. Even at age 50.

. . . Know the lay of the land.
More-seasoned workers know how their workplaces operate. They've figured out whether most promotions are based on creativity or attention to detail, sales or production/operations experience, computer or interpersonal skills. Then they work on the skills needed to capitalize on their workplace's culture.

. . . Create opportunities — and take responsibility.
Ideas are the lifeblood of the workplace. Consequently, 50-something workers constantly deliver well-researched ideas and then volunteer to take charge of their execution. Initiative is another way of saying you deserve to continue to succeed in your career.

. . . Become experts in their field.
Yogi Berra once said that you can learn a lot by watching. True enough. Watch and listen long enough and you could soon become an expert in your field. And nobody does that better than a 50-something career professional. Rather than sitting and waiting for someone to come along and proclaim them an expert, as too many workplace denizens do, these workers have long since learned to go out and become such experts.

Whether it's taking a class to learn Excel, writing for an industry trade magazine, or even offering to talk in front of a Chamber of Commerce group, 50-somethings won't hesitate — and more important aren't afraid — to become industry experts. Imagine giving a speech on manufacturing line innovations and noticing your CEO was in the audience? Becoming an expert is hard work for younger professionals — they don't have that same "lay of the land" knowledge that you do. Take advantage of that.

. . . Treat their careers as their own small businesses.
Older workers have learned over the years how to take control of their own careers. They don't like leaving things to chance. Like the neighborhood grocer or that software start-up out by the interstate, a 50-something career professional takes reputation and responsibilities personally. And there's no greater value to a company than someone who solves problems fast.

. . . Know their industry cold.
More-experienced professionals can just about cite chapter and verse on what their industry is up to on a daily basis. That sounds tough, especially for ultra-busy people like single parents or professionals who volunteer in their communities. But all that is required to become savvy about your industry is reading the right trades and publications. Even better is developing your

own contacts in the industry and chatting them up once a week or so. The Web is a big help, too. Subscribe to an online "clipping" service that will e-mail you news and information on your business community. Lexis-Nexis (www.lexisnexis.com) and Northern Light (www.northernlight.com) are good places to start. So are Business Wire (www.businesswire.com) and PR Newswire (www.prnewswire.com). Take advantage of these resources.

. . . Know the value of being a mentor.
Invariably, a younger worker lines herself up with someone who can champion her progress inside the executive boardrooms. In a smaller business that may be the CEO or the office administrator. In larger businesses a mentor can be the director of your department — or another department — or simply a fellow coworker who's got the ear of company decision makers. In virtually all cases, that mentor is an older worker willing to share his or her knowledge and experience with younger protégés. Management loves mentors — shared knowledge means a more savvy workplace. That usually translates into larger profits and a successful company.

. . . Have developed a fat Rolodex.
Collecting business cards might seem like a waste of time to some people. But a more experienced worker knows that a phone number here or an e-mail address

there can come in handy down the road. Contacts also come in handy when looking for good information on your industry. While nobody likes a pest, one thing I've learned in business is that people love to talk if you give them a chance.

. . . Stay ahead of the education curve.

Let's face it. We're in a global economy now where information is as much a commodity as compact disks or convertibles. As technology changes seemingly on a daily basis, it's the savvy 50-something worker who keeps up. That could mean taking that class in Web design or simply chatting up your coworkers for the latest trends in commerce and technology. Think of it as business insurance.

. . . Recognize what they are worth.

Successful 50-something professionals always know their value to their company, to their industry, and to potential future employers. There's no shortage of surveys and annual reports on salaries in the workplace. Another good idea is to scout out the help-wanted ads (many include salary ranges these days) or contact a good recruiter. Such a person can tell you what you're worth on the open market.

...Take politics in stride.

Older workers know how to play office politics, and more important, they know they have to play office politics. They know how to communicate with everyone in the workplace, from the intern in the mailroom to the company president. Rather than feeling victimized over not getting a promotion, they focus on what they can learn from the situation. In that way, even their disappointments become stepping stones, not roadblocks.

Like fine wine, the best career professionals are the ones who age gracefully.

24

Stay curious, be relevant, and THRIVE!

**Sometimes, success locks people into ruts.
Three artists offer advice on how to remain
inspired after 50.**

BY DAVID EBONY

David Ebony is associate managing editor of *Art in America*
magazine. His most recent book, *Carlo Maria Mariani,* was
published by Volker Huber, Frankfurt, 2002.

The best artists inspire. That is, after all, part of
their job. They give us new ideas, new ideals, and
in some cases, a new sense of humor.

Recently, when facing the distress of turning 50, I
looked to artists in my age bracket for hope and inspira-
tion. Maybe they could help me deal with the daunting
uncertainties of middle age. I found the promise of
renewal, and more, in the stories of three of today's
most prominent and influential artists: Cindy Sherman,

Fred Wilson, and Ross Bleckner. The photo-artist, sculptor/installation artist, and the painter, respectively, are thriving, not merely surviving, as they settle into their 50s. All three are already internationally renowned for the sizable contributions they have made to contemporary art. Yet these innovators continue to explore a broad array of technical experimentation in their art, and touch upon a wide range of issues and themes, including identity, race, and sexuality. Today, they are at the pinnacle of their creative powers.

Photo-artist Cindy Sherman, who turned 50 in 2004, maintains a positive, inquisitive, and unassuming attitude about herself, her work, and her surroundings, which might seem unlikely for one who has been in the glaring and often unforgiving art-world spotlight for more than 20 years. She's confident and fearless enough to submerge her good looks further than ever in her most recent work, a stunning series of self-portraits in which she assumes the guises of outrageous and sometimes grotesque clowns. These colorful, large-scale images met with considerable acclaim in exhibitions in New York and London.

In pondering the notion of turning 50, Sherman doesn't look back. She has no interest in resting on her laurels, despite an extraordinarily successful career — one of those rare coincidences of critical respect and commercial appreciation (her works regularly sell in the six figures these days).

"I don't ever want to repeat myself," she says. "I can't be bored. I'd rather be apprehensive and unsure of what I'm doing in order to challenge myself."

She has myriad ambitions. A one-time Hollywood film director (*Office Killer,* 1998), she says, "I'd still like to write a script and direct another film of some sort, although it doesn't have to be feature length. I've been thinking of making some sculptural pieces, too, ever since I did sets for a dancer friend last year. I'd like to become more adept at using Photoshop [a computer program for artists and photographers] for fun and for work. I'm open to using it more in my work, but I'm just not sure how, except for backgrounds right now.

"I want to travel more, for fun rather than for work, and I'd like to get back to learning to play the piano."

Bumping into Fred Wilson during a gala opening of the new Museum of Modern Art in the fall of 2004, I brought up the question of his milestone birthday and his inclusion in this book. "I'm not sure how to respond. Now everyone will know I've turned 50!" He needn't worry. With his vivacious demeanor and dashing good looks — complete with stylish dreadlocks and mischievous, piercing eyes — he's obviously hit that magic number in exemplary style. And his career could not possibly be going better. Recently, he has received a great deal of attention for his elegant and penetrating installations, sculptures, and two-dimensional works.

In 2003, Wilson represented the United States at the ever-prestigious Venice Biennale. Appearing shortly after the U.S. invasion of Iraq, his sumptuous and generous presentation of large-scale sculptures, photo pieces, and installations, which filled the American pavilion, was a subtle-yet-impassioned plea for justice and tolerance. It was one of the Biennale's more thoughtful and profound displays. It focused on important racial issues, both in general terms and with regard to Italy's assimilation of African immigrants. And, as if attaining that career goal was not enough to sustain him, an extensive museum survey of his work, "Objects and Installations, 1979-2000," recently toured the U.S., appearing in eight major venues. During his 50th birthday year, the highly acclaimed show was on view at the Studio Museum of Harlem in New York, his hometown.

Ross Bleckner, born in 1949, remains one of the most charismatic personalities in the New York art scene. He embodies the notion that the 50s can be among the best and most fulfilling years of one's life. Over the years, he has contributed, by means of his expansive and elegiac canvases, a uniquely humanistic meditation on the AIDS crisis. He continues to paint haunting, macrocosmic and microcosmic images of ethereal spaces. Building upon his well-known vocabulary of forms, including birds, candles, and urns, his recent compositions feature clusters of blood-cell shapes, which address metaphysical concerns of the body, life, love, death, and transcendence. These have been featured in several recent well-received (and sold-out) shows at home and abroad.

Bleckner, usually surrounded by a posse of attractive young admirers, is at the top of his game. "In regards to being in my 50s, I feel grateful to be here and to be comfortable with myself and in good health," he says. "I aim to keep focused, accept limitations and keep things simple, or even simpler. It's important to be engaged with the world outside of myself yet stay in my own rhythm, no matter what. Not to become an 'older artist' is key. I want to stay curious and to be relevant. To be a person who can be happy a lot of the time without thinking that being happy is what it's all about. Getting over yourself already makes one happy. Make some kind of peace with yourself. Calm, focused, and clear is the new happy. Welcome to 50, the new 40."

Spending time with these talented artists helps me find a new sense of hope, as both settle into their 50s, at the peak of their professional and creative lives. ☼

25

Hire yourself

If you're passionate, competent, and have a good plan, 50-plus is an ideal time to start your own business.

BY ALAN WEISS

Alan Weiss is one of those rare people who can say he is a consultant, speaker, and author and mean it. His consulting firm, Summit Consulting Group Inc., has attracted clients such as Merck, Hewlett-Packard, GE, Mercedes-Benz, State Street Corporation, Times Mirror Group, the Federal Reserve, *The New York Times*, Avon, and more than 400 other leading organizations. He maintains a global coaching practice, and is the author of 36 books, including *Million Dollar Consulting* and *Thrive! Stop Wishing Your Life Away*.

In my line of business, entrepreneurs have always led the pack. And these days, there is no shortage of like-minded go-getters. More and more people are starting businesses at ages traditionally seen as the beginning of retirement, or starting down entirely new career paths.

Whether your reasons are downsizing, early retirement, disgust with others controlling your destiny, or a passion for a particular pursuit, there are some absolute imperatives required to succeed. So, no matter what your motivation, here are the "musts":

First, there must be a defined market for your services. That market may be pre-existing; it may be created (the Walkman led to the iPod, and people never expected they would ever need such a device); or anticipated (the need to manage virtual team members who never see each other). But you must define what need you are addressing or anticipating.

Second, you must have the competency not only to meet the need, but also to compete well against others who already do. That means that a hobby or avocation isn't enough unless you're truly distinctive in your approach, methodology, technology, and so forth. Starting a business to repair toy trains won't work if you're merely a dabbler and not an excellent electrician and metalworker. Similarly, beginning a sales consulting operation will not be very effective if you are a good sales person but have never been a sales trainer.

Third, you must have passion. Make no mistake; no matter the nature of your new enterprise, you're in the marketing business, too. You have to sell yourself and your business, and there will be a ton of rejection. Passion for your pursuit and your value will help overcome the inevitable disappointments and detours.

At 50, you have an unusual advantage. You have a wealth of experience to draw upon, have made most of your mistakes long ago, and probably have a great network and/or contact list. These are distinct advantages of "maturity."

And that brings us to the next step: Contact everyone you know. That's right, everyone. Make a list of friends, acquaintances, former colleagues, customers, vendors, professional associates, civic group contacts, etc. Send all of them an e-mail, a voice mail, or a conventional letter stating what you're now doing and asking if you can be of assistance to them and/or whether they can give you the names of people you might be able to assist. Networking is Job One. If you don't tell them, they won't know you're there or what you're doing. If you don't blow your own horn, there is no music.

In order to get your business off the ground, you'll need to develop a business plan (a blueprint to follow for your business) and a marketing plan (to attract customers) for your new business. A good business plan should explain what your business does, how duties are delegated, and how you are going to make money. Pretty standard stuff.

Marketing plans differ. If you're not sure how to create one, then just answer these three questions:

1. What is the value proposition you bring to market, expressed as a business outcome? (For example, training classes are not value propositions, but increased sales at lower cost of acquisition are.)

2. Who is the likely buyer who can actually write a check for that value? (It's probably not a training manager, but may well be the vice president of sales, which means that's the person to talk to.)

3. How do you reach and market to that buyer?

You should also invest in the following:
- Quality letterhead, business cards, and envelopes.
- A presentation folder and promotional material ("position papers," biographical sketches, references, typical client results, an array of services offered, etc.).
- A top-line computer and printer.
- A reliable cell phone and multi-line office phone.
- A very well-made suit that you wear only to new prospect meetings.
- Subscriptions to relevant literature (e.g., *The Wall Street Journal, Business Week*, etc.).

There's not a thing wrong with working from your home, but make sure you have privacy and room for your equipment. You'll probably also need a copier and fax machine, postage meter and scale, and filing space. (All of this is legitimately deductible on tax returns, by the way.)

Also, find a lawyer and an accountant who understand solo practice and small business, not your cousin Louie or the person who closed on your house. Incorporate immediately as an LLC, a Chapter C, or a Subchapter S (your accountant can tell you which is best for your circumstances). Acquire errors and omissions (malpractice) insurance, liability insurance, and disability insurance. Find a Web designer and start a Web site (or at least reserve the domain name).

Once again, those over 50 have some real advantages. We are far more credible as guest speakers. We've probably learned how to write decently to have articles published. We have the experience to make an interviewer interested in what we say. We belong to enough groups, past and present, to facilitate networking, and most likely have the requisite networking (also known as "schmoozing") skills.

And, most important, we probably have a slew of 50-plus colleagues and acquaintances who have risen to positions that constitute potential buying points for us. It's far easier for a mature person to establish a peer-to-peer buyer relationship with a contemporary.

So, the real secret may be to ignore the purported draw-backs of age and focus on the very real advantages:

- A long-developed network of professional relationships.
- An immediate peer rapport with buyers.
- The experience to draw on examples and anecdotes.
- The stature of an expert who has "been there and done that."
- At least a minimum of financial and other support resources required for business investment.
- Existing banking, legal, accounting, and other key relationships.

There is no time like the present for people over 50 to initiate and develop personal businesses, whether from need or from desire. Just remember, you face a marketing challenge, and people will not rush to your door. You must create the groundswell by building on the very history that has led you to where you are today. ☼

26

Stop proving yourself

Give yourself credit; you're a classic. You deserve to be able to relax a little and take in some of the things you've missed.

BY SUSAN SEIDELMAN

Susan Seidelman graduated from NYU Film School with a masters degree in the late 1970s. Her films include *Desperately Seeking Susan, Making Mr. Right, She-Devil, Boynton Beach Club* and the pilot episode of *Sex And The City.* Seidelman has also been nominated for Emmy® Awards as well as an Academy Award.

I'm a film director, and I'm over 50. For me, turning 40 was more difficult than turning 50. I work in an industry that is very youth-oriented, so going from being a filmmaker in my 30s to one in my 40s was the big leap. Once I was over that hurdle, turning 50 wasn't a big deal — I actually liked it. My son was born in my late 30s; prior to that, my time was spent with work. When I reached my 40s, I was all about family. By the time I turned 50, my son was becoming more self-sufficient, so now I'm all about getting back to being me — and the endless challenge of figuring out how to combine work and family, and finally achieving comfort with who I am now.

In the film industry, turning 50 is as much a gender issue as it is an age issue. The double whammy thing is going strong. In the film industry, people are always looking for the next new thing, whether that newest thing is the star or the director. But older directors like Martin Scorsese, Woody Allen, Francis Ford Coppola, and Brian de Palma are considered masters. You don't really have that equivalent when it comes to women. Why? Probably because there aren't that many women past 50 who have been able to accumulate a significant body of work — maybe that's because the industry just hasn't afforded women the same kind of opportunities.

I started out directing films over 25 years ago. *Desperately Seeking Susan* was my first studio movie. I remember in 1984 when I first walked onto that set, I was clearly one of the younger people, plus I was female, plus I was five feet tall. I probably looked like a P.A. (production assistant) — one of the crewmembers even asked me to get him a cup of coffee. Now, it's 20 years later, I just finished filming a movie in Florida, and when I walked onto that set I was referred to as "Mrs. Seidelman." I looked around . . . expecting to see my mother! I wasn't the oldest person in the crew, but I was now definitely one of the oldest.

What I really like about my age is that, professionally, I have less to prove now. I know what I know, I know what I'm good at, and I also know what I don't know — and I'm not afraid to ask questions. For example, there is all this new digital technology, computer-generated effects, digital editing, and other stuff that younger people take for granted. I'm not as familiar as some of the younger filmmakers with the new technology, but at this stage, I look at things differently: Technology is just a tool. Along with age comes more life experience, and I think I have more insight into people and storytelling than I did when I was 30. I look at technology simply as a tool to tell interesting stories on film.

A big part of being a director is working with actors. I actually feel that getting older is an advantage; it has given me more experience working with people, I'm more patient, and I've learned how to get what I need in any given situation. And there's another factor — being a mother has also helped; I've become more maternal, tolerant, and patient, and I use those skills when I collaborate with actors. Years of experience (and learning from my mistakes) have enabled me to get what I need without getting someone's back up, or making them feel insecure or defensive.

As a director, I am most interested in the stories that have adult protagonists who are dealing with contemporary adult issues. Also, my films tend to be mostly character-oriented and my interests sociological. I'm curious about how people deal with modern relationships — whether it's *Sex and the City* or *Desperately Seeking Susan*. The movie I just finished filming in Florida is set in an "adult" gated community and is about people in their 60s who suddenly find themselves single again and back in the "dating game" at this stage in their life — a time when they never expected to be dealing with that stuff again. I find it interesting that there are more and more "senior citizens" looking for love, companionship, and sex. More seniors are dating and living together. And with all the new "sexual enhancement" drugs on the market, more seniors are having sex.

The perception of getting older isn't what it used to be, now that the Baby Boomer generation is in its 50s and 60s. Think about it: Mick Jagger is a grandfather! The generation that were children in the 1950s, came of age in the 1960s, and are now in their 50s, will soon be approaching their 60s, and that will change the way we think about aging.

In terms of films as you enter your 50s, I would definitely recommend catching up on some of the great ones that you may have missed. My personal list of favorites includes *Citizen Kane, Lawrence of Arabia, Chinatown, Brief Encounter, Rebel Without a Cause,* and *North by Northwest.* I'd also recommend some great American movies from the 1960s and '70s, like *Raging Bull, The Godfather, Badlands, Midnight Cowboy, The Graduate, The Last Picture Show,* and *The Way We Were,* as well as some Billy Wilder films, like *The Apartment* or *Some Like it Hot;* and some Woody Allen films like *Manhattan, Broadway Danny Rose,* and *Radio Days.* I think everyone should see a Fellini film by the time they're 50 — my favorites are *Nights of Cabiria* and *Amacorde.* Other foreign films I'd recommend are François Truffaut's *The 400 Blows,* Hector Babenco's *Pixote,* Lina Wertmüller's *Seven Beauties,* John Boorman's *Hope and Glory,* and Bernardo Bertolucci's *Last Tango in Paris* and *The Conformist.*

Finally, I'd say the best thing about being 50 is that there is a kind of confidence that comes with age. Hopefully you've made peace with whatever direction your life has taken you, so there is no longer that pressure to have to prove anything to yourself or the world. ☀

27

Now that you're tops at what you do, teach

Once you've reached the apex of your game — whether you're a prima ballerina or a regional vice president — look for opportunities to pass it on to the young.

BY ELEANOR D'ANTUONO

Eleanor D'Antuono was a prima ballerina with American Ballet Theatre for over 20 years. She began her career with Ballet Russe de Monte Carlo and was the first American ballerina to appear as a guest artist with Kirov Ballet in Leningrad, as well as with Chinese companies. Since her retirement from active performing, she stages ballets for many companies and is on the faculty at the Joffrey Ballet School.

Turning 50 for me was painless — a fairly graceful transition, really. But I don't take credit for planning it that way; it just happened.

Throughout my career, even though I never formally taught classes, I was used to helping other dancers.

Somehow, I just became so busy with everyone else — with coaching, advising, staging for other companies — that I no longer had time to spend dancing the way I wanted. I can't say that I regret it; I'm not concerned about what I'm not doing because what I AM doing is very satisfying. This may be hard to understand because I loved performing. But now I am simply experiencing a different part of that world. So I am still enjoying my passion.

All my life, ballet has been my passion. I started taking lessons when I was four years old and began dancing professionally when I joined the Ballet Russe de Monte Carlo at 14. I danced with the Ballet Russe for years; I danced and studied with Robert Joffrey; and I danced for more than 20 years with American Ballet Theatre, which is where I made my name. I've had my own company, too. So dance has been my life.

Because ballet is an art form, it has no end. You never really accomplish it all; you reach a little further each time. Even when I teach, I think like that. Sometimes I get frightened — what if the day comes when I no longer have anything to offer? Dance is about continuing to grow, remaining current. So even though I'm not performing, I am still trying to be good at what I am doing.

Sometimes, I find it a shock not to be young anymore. I never thought about not being young, ever, and then, all of a sudden, one day I looked in the mirror, and even though I felt the same, I wasn't young. That was hard for me — but it's not something I dwell on. I still look good in my clothes. I'm very physical. I work out, I take ballet class, I do Pilates. And when I see my students, my young dancers, I appreciate how they look. I enjoy them for what they are, and even though I don't want to look like that little girl, being older doesn't mean you can't look appealing and attractive. Still, it's a different concept. And I believe you make yourself look better by being attractive as a human being.

I have loved my profession, and still love it, in every possible way. I work with professionals and young people, and there are a lot of challenges when you're teaching. I never thought I could be an outstanding teacher — what do I know about how to communicate? But the students think I know something — I try to explain to them there is no secret . . . So teaching and coaching has become my work, and it's very gratifying. ☼

Section Six

MASTERING
YOUR MONEY

28

Pay off your mortgage

Reduce your debt now, so that saving for the future won't be as difficult.

BY SUZE ORMAN

Suze Orman, an Emmy award-winning author, talk show host, magazine columnist, writer/producer, and motivational speaker, has been called a "one-woman financial advice powerhouse" and "a force in the world of personal finance" by *USA Today.* She has been able to translate her own experiences — from the stress of her father's losing his business to her post-college job as a waitress to her climb up the ranks in the investment world — into frank, savvy financial advice that has transformed the lives of millions around the world.

I n your 50s, instead of panicking about the income you need to build up in the next 15 or 20 years, your best move is to concentrate on getting your costs down. If you will need less to live on in retirement, then you won't need to risk desperate accumulation strategies now. Right? That's a pretty basic point that everyone seems to miss.

I want you to make cost reduction Plan A in your Late-Start Retirement Strategy. And the single biggest cost you can eliminate is your mortgage. If you live in a house you intend to stay in, your best move right now is to get your loan paid off ASAP.

I know, I know. You're thinking, "Suze, are you crazy? My house is my only tax break!" For many of you that means you are getting just 25 to 30 cents back for every dollar you pay in interest. Feel free to double-check my math, but I believe that still leaves 70 to 75 cents coming out of your pocket. This is not really saving money; all you are doing is reducing your *current* monetary outflow. At the same time, you aren't making much progress paying off your loan. You do realize, don't you, that on a 30-year mortgage you will have paid off just 25 percent or less of the principal after 15 years? You've been making payments for 15 years and most of it was interest.

Stop drinking the mortgage-interest-deduction Kool-Aid. If you are getting a late start on your retirement investing, getting that mortgage paid off ASAP is going to give you the best, safest return for your money, not to mention great peace of mind.

Let's say you have a 30-year fixed-rate mortgage with 25 years left on it. The $200,000 mortgage carries a 6 percent interest rate, which brings your basic mortgage costs (not including property tax and insurance) to

$1,200. You're going to be on the hook for that $1,200 a month until you are 70. Chances are, you don't want to keep working at 70 (or even if you did, you might find it hard to keep a high-paying job); so that $1,200 is going to be a big ticket to have to punch when you're no longer pulling in a strong monthly paycheck.

Now let's play my favorite game, called *What If.*

What if you can't keep working past 65? At 65 you get laid off and can't land a job at similar pay. There's no pension because fewer and fewer companies give them out these days. All you've got is your 401(k) assets. And don't be counting on the option of taking early Social Security benefits at 62.

All these glum facts mean that for a few more years you'll need to rely on your 401(k) to do the heavy lifting of supporting you, including paying that $1,200 monthly mortgage.

Clearly your 401(k) is not the best solution to your retirement quandary. Can we please consider my better idea? Get your mortgage paid off before you retire.

I want you to continue contributing to your 401(k) each year to get your maximum company match. That's free money you shouldn't pass up. Not all employers offer a company match, but I will assume you have a super great employer who gives you a 50 percent match up to

$2,000 a year. That would mean you need to contribute $4,000 to get that $2,000. But after that amount, I want you to stop your contributions and use the money to pay down your mortgage. If you contribute just $4,000 next year, rather than the $13,000 that you alone were contributing, that would free up $9,000 to pay down your mortgage. Adjusted for a typical tax bite, that's still about $540 a month you would have available to add to your mortgage payment.

Okay, hang in there, we're almost done. Remember we started with a 30-year mortgage that has 25 years left on it, so it won't be paid off until you, our 50-year-old, will be 75. But by making that extra $540 payment each month, you can pay off the mortgage in about 12.5 years — when you are just 63. Two years before you retire/get laid off, you own your house free and clear. No more $1,200 a month to stress over.

And you still have two years until D-day, when you get laid off. If during that stretch you took all the money you used to pay on the mortgage — the $1,200 plus your extra $540 a month — you would have nearly $44,000 saved up after two years, assuming you earned 5 percent on the money.

We'll come back to this $44,000 chunk of change in a moment. First I want to remind you that while you

were paying off your house quickly you were still contributing to your 401(k). For 15 years you had a total
of $6,000 going into the account annually ($4,000 was
yours, and $2,000 was a company match). Assuming a 7
percent annual rate, you're looking at having more than
$158,000. Add in the $44,000 and you're over $200,000.
You have your mortgage completely paid off and you
still managed to save a bit more than half of what you
would have if you had stuck solely to the 401(k) investing plan.

And I just want to anticipate the flurry of letters that
will say if you took your savings from the mortgage
interest deduction and invested it, you could build up a
savings account that would exceed my idea. Maybe yes,
maybe no. But are you really going to tell me that after
procrastinating about retirement for 20 years, someone
is going to have the wherewithal to know what they are
saving on the mortgage interest deduction and invest it
each month? Come on.

29

Bulk up your portfolio's defense

Make sure your money keeps growing, even when the markets don't.

BY BILL GROSS

Bill Gross is the founder and co-CIO of PIMCO and oversees nearly $1 trillion in securities. He is the portfolio manager of the world's largest mutual fund, the PIMCO Total Return Fund. Gross is the first money manager to have been named Morningstar's Fixed Income Manager of the Year and Morningstar's first Fixed Income Manager of the Decade.

Home runs, slam-dunks, and go-for-broke downfield passes are the highlight moments in professional sports, but every coach will tell you it's defense that wins championships.

When it comes to investing, having a good defense means protecting your portfolio against potential pitfalls so that your money grows despite the inevitable market swings. So, what are those pitfalls and how do you defend your portfolio against them?

I believe that one of the biggest long-term risks investors face is the potential for rising inflation . . . and at the end of the day, isn't one of the goals of investing to increase your ability to buy things in the future? Rising inflation means the dollars you invest today will buy fewer "things" in the future. Sure, inflation hasn't been much of a threat in recent decades, but as the saying goes, and the attorneys will like this line: "Past performance is no guarantee of future results."

What's happening is that there is an ongoing battle in the United States and global economies between the forces of inflation and the forces of deflation . . . and believe it or not, the biggest inflationary force today is the U.S. government. You see, the United States faces enormous debts, and the typical government response to huge debts is not to meet them but to inflate them away. The United States has been using its printing press to print mountains of dollars in an effort to do just that.

Deflationary forces, including cheap imports from China and the developed world's aging population, are strong as well. I don't know who will ultimately win, but in the past, the government and its printing press have been the victors . . . so I'd suggest bulking up your inflation defense. And you know what, turning 50 is a darn good milestone at which to take another look at your portfolio to ensure that you are adequately protected against inflation.

A second significant long-term risk facing investors right now is the potential for a decline in the U.S. standard of living. The United States consumes too much, and we pay for it with debt and a heavy dose of the rest of the world's savings, which they lend us so we can buy more of their stuff. Nevertheless, there will be a point when other nations will no longer be willing to subsidize our excesses . . . and it appears that we might be at that point right now.

Bottom line is that there is no easy fix for this imbalance in the global economy. For Americans to begin voluntarily to get "that old time religion" of saving more money is but a dream. And it seems equally unlikely that the government will be willing and/or able to move back to a balanced budget any time soon. As I noted earlier, the easiest solution, but not my preferred solution, is for the government to weaken the dollar and inflate the debt away.

The problem with this solution is that rising inflation, a declining dollar, and increasing overseas competition are all threats to the lifestyle that Americans enjoy today. As the dollar depreciates, the U.S. standard of living goes down. For example, as the value of the dollar falls, it's not just the trip to Europe you're planning that becomes more expensive, but all the imports that you buy become more expensive, too. So, a 50-year-old (or anyone for that matter) has to defend against not only domestic inflation but also the risk of a declining standard of living in the United States compared to the rest of the world.

There are two steps you can take to defend your portfolio against these threats. First, invest in bonds that are protected against inflation, namely U.S. Treasury inflation-indexed securities, or "TIPS." TIPS can help defend your portfolio against inflation because these securities are protected one-for-one against a rise in consumer prices. When consumer prices rise, the U.S. Treasury adjusts the principle and interest on TIPS upward to counteract the inflationary effect. These securities should be a core holding for investors of all ages. Commodities and other physical assets, such as real estate, can also offer some protection against inflation, but the average 50-year-old investor should carefully consider the higher risk that these investments can entail . . . the attorneys will like that caveat, too.

The second step is to diversify your investments globally. Americans are just beginning to understand that a portion of their portfolio should be spread around to diversified markets as well as diversified currencies. Europeans understand this because, prior to the advent of the euro, they had to trade and travel between countries using multiple currencies. They get it. Canadians understand this because they are one of America's largest trading partners . . . the continuing struggle between the looney and the buck. They get it. Americans, except during that spring-break trip to Cancun, don't really run into daily currency issues . . . so we're just on the brink of "getting it." Should the dollar continue to decline, American investors will come to understand the importance of global diversification — especially when they review their next quarterly statement. So, I'd recommend diversifying both currency-wise and market-wise.

When your offense goes flat, when the long bomb falls incomplete or the slam-dunk incredibly bounces off the rim, then a coach looks to his defense to hold the line. Bulk up your defense by buying some inflation protection and diversifying globally . . . and if you do, the only thing you'll have to fret about . . . is turning 60 . . . arggggh!!!

30

Rethink your insurance strategy

From life insurance to long-term care, the rules are different at midlife.

BY RICHARD BOWREN

Richard Bowren, one of State Farm Agency's top-producing insurance agents, is based in Doylestown, Pennsylvania, and has been helping clients meet their insurance needs for 15 years.

Insurance is serious business. There is an old joke in the industry about an agent who worked hard to sell a potential client a policy. "Don't let me frighten you into making a hasty decision, Mr. Fishbein," summed up the agent. "If you wake up tomorrow, call me."

Insurance of all kinds is one of the necessary evils that we have to deal with in life. No one wants to run into a circumstance that requires insurance coverage, but occasionally life dishes up a batch of lemons, and insurance provides an opportunity to make lemonade.

When tackling insurance issues, the first thing to do is work with a professional to have a comprehensive review of all your insurance programs. He or she can help you determine if you've got adequate — or maybe even too much — coverage in your auto, homeowners, life, health, and disability insurance programs. It is extremely important that both spouses have a full understanding of all coverages, why the coverage is in place, and whom to contact in the event of a question or a claim.

As we turn 50, we need to spend time evaluating our health insurance needs. Health insurance is not just for accidents and sickness; it also includes long-term care (LTC) and disability insurance.

Long-term care insurance is meant to protect your assets and allow you to maintain your freedom should you be unable to take care of yourself due to an injury or illness. Take a closer look at your disability coverage, and be sure to look at your current income and benefits. Will your benefits cover monthly expenses? Are taxes included? Once you retire, will your policy pay the benefits promised? If the benefits are not sufficient, can you purchase more?

As you have grown older, your assets have probably grown as well, thus creating the need for higher limits of liability protection. The cost of increasing liability limits is very small compared to the amount of coverage you can add to your present policy. It's important to make sure that your liability limits adequately protect your assets, reducing your overall risk of exposure in case of accident or lawsuit.

Life insurance is an important subject to those who are turning 50. For some, many risks and financial obligations are behind us, mortgages may be lower or eliminated, children's educations may be paid for, and savings plans have had time to build to the point of being able to generate income if needed. For others, those obligations are still ahead. Whatever type of life insurance policies you own, be sure your beneficiaries are current and up-to-date. Unfortunately, this is very easily overlooked, but you want to be sure the benefits will be distributed according to your wishes.

If your employer is supplying any or all of your life insurance coverage, find out if the coverage is convertible. (If it isn't, you will lose it when you leave the company, and replacing it isn't always easy, especially if you've had health issues.)

Taking a closer look at your auto insurance can also be helpful. It isn't always wise to opt for the minimum medical coverage provided with your auto insurance policy. Make sure you ask about the price differences, what is covered, what coverage is primary, and the benefits your health insurance provides for injuries in an automobile accident. You may be able to save money on your comprehensive and collision coverage, which pays for repairs of physical damage to your vehicle. Because your assets have grown, you can probably reduce your premiums substantially by accepting more risk and taking a higher deductible in this area.

The same thinking applies to your home insurance. Do you have adequate liability? Keep in mind that, while your homeowner's insurance policy covers your home and possessions, the policy is also the primary source of your personal liability protection. The coverage typically follows you wherever you go. For example, if you are on a golf course and accidentally injure someone or damage property while there and are found liable for those damages, your homeowner's insurance will pay for your defense and indemnification costs.

A major lawsuit could wipe out your entire savings, so you want to be certain to have adequate coverage. An excellent way to be sure you won't be financially ruined by a lawsuit is to purchase a liability umbrella policy. This policy is fairly inexpensive and adds a significant amount of coverage to your auto and home liability coverage.

As for your home and its contents, does your policy cover your home's current replacement value? Ask your agent to revalue your home and check to see that your policy is adequate. Does your policy cover your treasured items? Do you want them covered? What is the best way to replace them if they are destroyed or stolen? Do you have current documentation on what you own, including photos, receipts, and records?

Once you've taken the time to assess your current levels of insurance coverage and the changes in your assets and life situation, you'll have a clearer understanding of where you can cut back on insurance costs and where you need to supplement your coverage. It's important not to underestimate the importance of insurance as you plan for the future — it can mean the difference between financial hardship and financial peace of mind. ☀

31

Strengthen your will

No more excuses: Your family needs the protection that comes from a clear, up-to-date last will and testament.

BY REBECCA SMOLEN

Rebecca Smolen is a partner in WolfBlock's Private Client Services Practice Group. She concentrates her practice in the areas of tax and estate planning, closely held business succession planning, charitable giving, estate and trust administration, and tax-exempt organizations. Smolen has authored numerous articles and lectures frequently on various topics related to her practice areas.

While many people find estate planning complex, the idea behind it is simple: to control your assets during your lifetime while also leaving a legacy to those people and institutions you care about most. Having an estate plan in place is one of the most important steps you can take on behalf of your family and/or your business.

First, it is crucial that you select an executor or trustee for your estate. You need to find a person you can trust with the administration of your estate and the administration of any trusts you create for your heirs. This can be a person or a bank or trust company, but it must be someone who you feel comfortable will abide by your wishes.

It is also important to name people to handle your financial and health care affairs if you are unable. This means executing a general power of attorney, health care power of attorney, and living will. For a living will, it is important to determine your feelings on the administration of life-sustaining medical treatment (including nutrition and hydration) in the event you are terminally ill, permanently unconscious, or suffering from another impaired health condition where the benefits of life may be outweighed by its burdens.

If you have children under 18, be sure you have identified guardians should you and the other parent die before they reach legal adult age (18 in most states). Also, consider what resources and assets will be available to your children and spouse if you die before your children become adults.

Next, calculate your net worth (assets plus life insurance death benefits, less liabilities). Make sure you consider potential future inheritances from parents and/or others when estimating this figure. If your total net worth exceeds $1,000,000, be sure to consult with an estate planning attorney who is an expert in federal estate tax planning (under federal estate tax laws, the federal estate tax may come into play if you die with more than $1,000,000, in which case federal estate tax rates can be as high as 55 percent). In this situation your estate planning documents should be structured to minimize the estate tax hit; you may want to consider a structured gifting program to reduce the amount of your estate that will ultimately be subject to taxation.

Regardless of your net worth, you must evaluate what portions of your estate you wish to be divided among your spouse, children, charities, and others. Additionally, you need to decide whether money for individuals (i.e. spouse, children, or others) should be given outright or in trust, keeping in mind various protection issues for your heirs and "affluenza" issues (i.e. when children inherit enough money so they don't have to work and may get themselves in trouble with "idle hands").

If your parents are living, talk to them about whether they've addressed the issues above, and if not, make a priority of helping them get their affairs in order. If they have, get a sense of how they have set up their affairs and evaluate whether your financial situation should impact how they plan their estates. For example, if you are very well-off, it may make sense for them to set aside your "share" of their assets for your children, being mindful of federal generation skipping tax issues. If you have creditor issues (i.e., if you are a doctor who is concerned about medical malpractice claims), it may be wise to suggest they put your inheritance in trust so it is inaccessible to creditors.

The issues surrounding inheritance are particularly important to the Baby Boomer generation. Baby Boomers are stepping into the largest inheritance ever, some $10.4 trillion in total. On average, they're expected to receive around $90,000 each, with the top 10 percent of inheritors taking in a cool half-million each. But unfortunately, experts say, boomers are largely unprepared. In many cases, parents — who've put a lot of effort into setting aside a bequest — haven't given the actual transfer of wealth a great deal of thought, either.

That can be a costly mistake. Inheritances can be frittered away by mismanagement, lost to estate taxes, or drained by court battles. So how do you make the most of an inheritance? Here are a few tips:

• *Do nothing.* Not forever, of course, but for the first six months to a year, stash any money you receive in a safe haven — such as a money-market or certificate-of-deposit account — and do little else. Keep going to work. Keep your spending in check. Why? There's a temptation to splurge to avoid the reality that you've lost a loved one. If you're able to go through the grieving process first, you have a much better chance of making good financial decisions later.

• *Look at your debts first.* Before investing or spending any money you receive, consider whether it makes more sense to use it to pay down existing credit card or other debt.

• *Hire help.* For bequests of $20,000 or more, it's wise to have a financial adviser to make sure you make the best use of it. If you receive more than $250,000, you need an entire team: a lawyer, a financial planner, a broker, an insurance agent, and an accountant. Conduct interviews to find the right people.

Whatever you do, don't wait to take control of your estate planning. You'll find that you will look to the future with greater security and confidence, and your family will thank you for your efforts. ☀

32

Budget to your 100th birthday

The odds of your making it another 50 years are better than ever. Here's what you need to know to make sure you can live well, not just long.

BY ERIC FRIEDMAN

Eric Friedman is a retirement consulting actuary for Watson Wyatt Worldwide. He holds the designations of Fellow of the Society of Actuaries, Enrolled Actuary, Member of the American Academy of Actuaries, and Chartered Financial Analyst.

The lifestyles of people over 50 have changed dramatically over the last 100 years. Before 1900, retirement was virtually unheard of. Most people worked their entire adult lives, and the few who did retire did not need the extensive financial preparations necessary today, due to shorter life expectancies.

But these days, with increased longevity and retirement more common, financial planning has become challenging. Although life expectancy has increased only modestly relative to total lifespan, it is a huge increase when viewed as a percentage of life expectancy beyond the average retirement age. In 1940, the average life expectancy of a 65-year-old was 12.7 years for males and 14.7 for females. By 2040, those figures are projected to be 18.6 and 21.7 years respectively, representing a 50 percent increase in life expectancy. Since about half the population will outlive the average life expectancy, people should plan on saving enough to support themselves many years beyond their average life expectancy.

The trend of opting for earlier retirement compounds the challenge. As modern medicine improves the health and quality of life of elderly people, it would be possible to delay retirement — but this hasn't been the case. In fact, people are retiring earlier than they used to. In 1950, 46 percent of men over age 65 were in the workforce; by the mid-1990s, that figure fell to only 16 percent. Put simply, tomorrow's retirees will need to save much more than yesterday's retirees. In addition, in the past, children commonly became self-sufficient by the late teens; however, many parents now support their children through college and graduate school.

This continuing financial burden erodes the ability of some 50-year-olds to save for retirement.

The traditional model for retirement income is the "three-legged stool": Social Security, employer-sponsored pension plans, and personal savings (the amount you put into your retirement savings, usually through stock, bond, and mutual fund investments, and investments in tax-deferred vehicles like 401(k) plans and IRAs). By combining the "replacement ratio" — the proportion of post-retirement income to pre-retirement earnings — and the three-legged stool, we can form a simple model for retirement income needs. To maintain pre-retirement lifestyle, a common rule of thumb is that income from all three legs of the stool should total at least 70-80 percent of pre-retirement income. (The target replacement ratio is usually less than 100 percent because retirees have lower expenses: lower taxes, no need to save for retirement, no work-related expenses such as commuting costs, etc.)

1. *Social Security.* This program was never designed to be the sole source of retirement income for most people, though some retirees have used it that way. Social Security was intended to be a financial safety net, providing benefits closer to minimum subsistence levels. Although legislative changes to Social Security are debated, the expected benefit amount upon retire-

ment probably will not change much. Go to the Social Security Administration's Web site at http://www.ssa.gov to calculate your estimated benefits.

2. *Employer-sponsored pension plans.* The benefit levels of pension plans vary, but government employees and those who have stayed in their jobs generally receive better benefits. Recently, many employers have overhauled their pension plans; make sure you understand your benefits from every previous employer, and contact them if you're not sure what you're entitled to.

3. *Personal savings.* This is the area where you have the most control, but there is no simple formula to determine how much you should save. The primary rule is simply that the assets should be sufficient to generate the remainder of the income you need for retirement. A person with an average or below-average employer-sponsored pension plan will need more personal savings than someone with more generous employer-provided benefits.

All three legs of the stool should be considered during financial planning; otherwise the stool will become wobbly. One challenge is that some benefits are stated as annuity amounts, payable for life (e.g., $1,000 monthly pension); and others as single-sum account balances (e.g., $100,000 in a 401(k) account). It can be difficult to project total future savings, since one is stated as a lump sum and the other as periodic income. Compounding the problem is that investment returns can fluctuate significantly, and adjustments must be made for inflation, taxes, and your uncertain life expectancy.

As times change, the concept of retirement is also evolving. The traditional three-legged stool has been growing a fourth leg: income from part-time work after a person retires from his or her primary job. Research on phased retirement done by Watson Wyatt Worldwide shows an increasing number of people are transitioning into retirement gradually, slowly reducing the hours they work, instead of leaving the workforce abruptly.

Broad demographic trends are also likely to have a significant, and possibly negative, impact on society. Three major trends — decreasing fertility rates, increasing life expectancy, and the retirement of the Baby Boomer generation — will dramatically boost the number of retirees per worker. In the United States, the Social Security Administration estimates that the number of beneficiaries per 100 workers is expected to increase from 30 in 2003 to 46 in 2030 — an increase of more than 50 percent. Most nations in the developed world are facing similar situations.

Some speculate that these demographic trends foreshadow too few workers in the developed world to produce the goods society demands. Others hypothesize that as the proportion of people saving assets for retirement declines and the proportion of people selling assets to fund their retirement increases, prices of stocks and bonds may plummet. The combination of worker shortages and declining asset markets could force later retirement ages for typical workers because they will need to work longer to fund their retirement. Globalization and increases in economic productivity will be able to make up part of the shortfall, but if these measures fail to improve the financial situation sufficiently, the overall standard of living will likely decline.

There's an old Spanish proverb that says, "He who does not look ahead remains behind." Fortunately, financial planning tools allow us to look into the future more clearly, which gives proactive 50-somethings the ability to plan and save for a more financially secure future.

33

Get smart about the IRS

Paying taxes is inevitable, but it can hurt less than you think.

BY BRADFORD HALL, CPA

As the managing director of his own firm, Hall & Company, Bradford Hall is actively involved in all aspects of taxation, auditing, and business planning. He has more than 33 years of experience in public accounting. In addition, Hall spends a great deal of time consulting in the area of business management, business succession planning, estate planning, and preparation of comprehensive personal financial plans.

You have to admire the Internal Revenue Service. Any organization that makes that much money without advertising deserves our respect.

And respect it we must, especially when we turn the magic age of 50 and have to lay out a financial plan for the rest of our lives. Tax planning is a critical part of such a plan, encompassing a wide array of financial planning issues. Fortunately, there is a clear path to tax planning.

Below, I have outlined a few guidelines that will help you insure against risks and protect your ability to retire in style. Many people fail to insure against risks until it is too late. Life insurance should be taken out when a person is still healthy, by age 50 if you are lucky. The same applies to long-term care insurance.

The IRS allows specific tax breaks for you once you attain the magical age of 50 which you should give great consideration to. You are entitled to higher deductible retirement options called "catch-up contributions." For 2010 you are eligible to contribute an additional $1,000 catch up each year into your IRA, in addition to the regular $5,000 contribution.

If you participate in your company's SIMPLE IRA, and you are 50 or over you are able to contribute an additional $2,500 each year into the plan, in addition to the maximum $11,500. If you participate in a 401-K at work and are 50 or over you can contribute an additional $5,500 in addition to the maximum $16,500 in 2010. People who will turn 50 before the end of the tax year are generally permitted to make these additional deferrals.

If you are self-employed, you might consider a SEP (Simplified Employee Pension) or a Solo 401-K.

While you may have already talked about long-term care insurance with your insurance agent, there are tax benefits to these products designed to protect your assets if you are disabled by a chronic physical or mental illness. The Health Insurance Portability and Accountability Act of 1996 (HIPAA) encourages consumers to buy long-term care (LTC) insurance through tax deduction incentives for premiums and exclusions from income for benefits received. These incentives were offered to decrease the growing burden of long-term healthcare placed on Medicare and Medicaid.

Medicare will pay for up to 100 days of care in a qualified skilled nursing facility following a hospital stay of at least three consecutive days. However, Medicare is designed for skilled medical and nursing care of acute illnesses, not long-term custodial care for chronic, disabling physical or mental illnesses.

Medicaid pays for long-term care, but only if the person in need of care is impoverished — in most cases, single patients can have no more than $2,000 in nonexempt resources. In addition, a person must contribute a sizable portion of his or her income toward the cost of care.

The National Association of Insurance Commissioners (NAIC) in *A Shopper's Guide to Long-Term Care Insurance* warns that people should not consider buying LTC insurance if they cannot afford the premiums, have limited assets, receive only Social Security benefits or Supplemental Security Income (SSI) as income, and have trouble paying for utilities, food, medicine, or other important needs. The NAIC recommends people consider buying LTC insurance if they have significant assets and income to protect, can afford to pay for their own care, and don't want to be dependent on others.

Certain Social Security benefits are available upon reaching age 50. A surviving spouse is entitled to survivor's benefits if the deceased worker was fully insured and the surviving spouse is at least 65, or 50 and disabled, and married to the worker for at least nine months prior to the worker's death or is the parent of the worker's natural or adopted child. The surviving spouse can collect full benefits at age 65, but he or she can elect to receive reduced benefits beginning as early as age 60 (or 50 and disabled).

In this day and age, turning 50 is no big deal. As they say in all the self-help books, 50 is the new 30. And once you reach that milestone, you still have a long way to go — and a lot to prepare for. That's especially true when it comes to your taxes and your financial affairs. Get going today and ensure financial comfort in your golden years. ☀

Embrace your inner Trump

Why 50 is the perfect time to invest in real estate.

BY JO-ANNE ATWELL

Jo-Anne Atwell, a licensed real estate agent, is with Lisa James Otto Country Properties in New Hope, Pennsylvania, and is a member of the Pennsylvania Association of Realtors and the Bucks County Board of Realtors. Before earning her real estate license, Jo-Anne was business development manager for NovaCare Rehabilitation in Philadelphia.

Real estate is all about opportunity, and it's especially suited to those hitting the 50-year mark. In fact, you are at the perfect point in life to capitalize on this valuable market. At this stage in life, you've probably been a homeowner for years, if not decades. And you have enough assets or equity saved up to be able to consider the purchase of real estate as a serious addition to your investment portfolio. Younger people are less likely to have your asset base, and older people don't have the luxury of time.

Let's look first at the investment property market. According to the U.S. Census Bureau, 75 percent of multifamily investors are over the age of 45. More than half of these (51.6 percent) own fewer than five units, and they earned approximately 31 percent of their income from ownership of rental properties.

Surprised? Don't be: Most real estate investors come to the market later in life because they are concerned about their retirement and are at their highest potential earning power. Some have inherited money or real estate.

There are four major reasons that an investor might choose real estate for investment:

1. *Cash flow:* Yes, it is still possible in some parts of the country to get monthly cash from your investments. With the right choice of property, it is possible to have funds returned to the investor after all other expenses (mortgage, vacancy factor, repairs, property management, etc.) have been covered. Most banks will not lend money to buy a property if there is no hope of a cash-flow return.

2. *Appreciation:* Loosely applying the rules of supply and demand, we can rest assured that with our current immigration patterns as well as our population growth,

there will be a continued need for housing over the next 50 years. You can safely assume a 4 percent appreciation level. Of course, some years will be better than others.

The average single-family home sold for $23,400 in 1970; in 2000, a similar average home sold for $169,000. That is approximately an 8 percent annual increase. Appreciation will vary with the location and condition of the property.

3. *Equity buildup:* You reduce your mortgage and increase your equity with every mortgage payment made on underlying debt. A portion of your payment goes toward reducing the principal. The shorter the loan period, the faster the equity builds.

4. *Tax savings:* Uncle Sam allows everyone but brokers in real estate to depreciate investment properties on Schedule E when filing annual tax returns. Residential properties depreciate over 27.5 years and commercial properties over 39 years.

You may be ready to jump at all of these opportunities to make money. Bear in mind, though, that the government needs to pay its bills, and it gets its share when you sell one of your investments. When you sell a property, you will be faced with a 15 percent to 28 percent capital gains tax on the increase in value of the property and the recapture of the depreciation. This cost can be deferred if you complete a 1031 tax deferred exchange to trade up from property to property.

But the rewards can be sweet. Here's an example of a typical investment — a $340,000 townhouse, with a $150,000 down payment. At an interest rate of 6 percent, the monthly mortgage is $1,518, including taxes. (There's also a townhouse association fee of $133; insurance costs $60 per month.) Repairs on such a property, like staining the deck, are minimal. At about $2,400 a month, the rent more than covers expenses. Recently, a similar property sold for $400,000, so in one year, the value of the investment appreciated more than $60,000.

A heads-up, though: You can lose money in real estate, especially if the market slows down, if the economy goes sour, or if you're hit with a devastating illness, job loss, or any mishap that means you'll need quick cash. The key is balance — have enough cash on hand to cover any losses on your property. In real estate, liquidity is king.

To get started, pick an investment that will give you a chance to make some small mistakes, maybe your grandmother's duplex. Choose a real estate agent who has some of his or her own investments and a property management company with good references.

If you hate the idea of being someone's landlord, another

way to invest is by purchasing a second home. The U.S. second-home market is gearing up for what is virtually certain to be a series of record years for sales. And new research suggests that many more buyers are jumping into that market to make money, not to spend weekends at the beach sipping margaritas.

Whereas just 20 percent of second-home buyers in the beginning of the year 2000 were motivated primarily by investment returns, nearly double that number (37 percent) now rank rental income as their primary objective. The study defined "investment" properties as those rented out for six or more months per year and rarely if ever used personally by the owners. Traditional "non-investment" second homes, by contrast, are primarily purchased for personal use and only sporadically rented out.

Just who are these new, investment-minded Baby Boomers snapping up resort condos and homes? The typical purchaser is 56 years old, married with no children under age 18 or living at home, and relatively affluent, with an average household income of $92,000. Nearly 30 percent of all buyers expect to convert their second homes into their primary homes sometime in the future.

For example, a married couple in their mid-50s right

now could buy a second home in a resort community, rent it out for the next five to seven years, then sell their principal home tax-free, and convert the rental home to their new residence. That would start the tax clock ticking again on their resort residence and allow them to pocket all gains on the house tax-free (up to the $500,000 limit) after just 24 months of ownership and use.

So, consider real estate very carefully when thinking about your long-term financial and residential goals. The payoff could be much greater than you ever imagined. ☼

Give something back

**You know how to earn it; you know how to spend it.
But do you know how to give it away?**

BY LORNA WENDT

Lorna Wendt is the founder of Equality in Marriage
Institute, as well as the founding benefactor and board
member of the Women's Philanthropy Institute. She serves
on the advisery boards of Outward Bound USA, and the
University of Wisconsin's School of Music and College
of Letters and Sciences. In 2001, *Worth* Magazine named
Wendt one of the 10 most influential people in shaping the
way Americans view money.

I have found the fifth decade of my life to be a rewarding time of great self-discovery. I have been able
to take all the experiences and resources garnered
during my life and use them to accomplish my dreams
and make my personal agenda for change a reality.

After more than 30 years of marriage to the CEO
of General Electric Capital, during which I worked
to support my husband's education, maintained our

household, and raised our children, I faced divorce with a small settlement offer of 10 percent of our household assets. While the offer was a significant amount of money, I felt that accepting it would compromise my principles and disregard my role as an equal partner in our marriage. I decided to fight back by filing for divorce first. I put together a stellar team of legal and financial advisers. And I called *The Wall Street Journal.* A year before my divorce, my fairly predictable existence as a household manager and corporate supporter would not have allowed me to imagine the things that would follow. Our divorce truly became the "split heard 'round the world." From the cover of *Fortune* to *20/20* to *Oprah,* I found myself defending the whole concept of equality in marriage.

In the end, I was awarded 50 percent of our hard assets, and I had started a national dialogue on the value of stay-at-home spouses and the concept of equal partnerships. There I was, a 54-year-old woman on the other side of a precedent-setting divorce, wondering, "What do I do now?" As tempting as it might have been to step out of the spotlight, I felt I was on the cusp of fully discovering my potential and using my experiences to make a difference.

Philanthropy has always been an important part of my life. As the daughter of a minister, I was raised to be benevolent, help others, and try to make the world a better place. Charity is also a very important part of being the wife of a corporate leader and, throughout my marriage, I was involved in many different causes. After my divorce, I made it my mission to use my resources to make a difference and create change in the areas that were most important to me. And I learned very quickly the difference between simply being philanthropic and truly finding and establishing one's voice by helping others and taking steps toward accomplishing one's goals.

What I did was to take the lessons I learned and some of the money, and I founded The Equality in Marriage Institute. This philanthropic endeavor is a nonprofit organization that encourages men and women to actively manage their partnerships to make them stronger, healthier, and more balanced. It also provides information, resources, and support to help people build, maintain and, if necessary, dissolve their partnerships and marriages. It also helps people facing divorce educate themselves so they can handle the emotional and financial transitions.

Education and helping people obtain the skills they need to manage and empower their lives have become a primary focus of my philanthropic voice.

Instead of donating small amounts of money and time to a long list of diverse causes, I found it more satisfying and life-affirming to focus more of my time and resources on the causes most important to me. And in embracing philanthropy, not just by writing checks but also by creating my own personal agenda, I learned that I could use my voice and resources to make a difference in the world. This can work for anyone.

The following tips can help each of you use your life's journey to create your own philanthropic voice and empower yourself by helping others and improving the world around you.

Think About It
No matter our occupation or life's experiences, we have all been involved with issues or situations that made us form opinions or want to do something to create change. Regardless of what the media or those around you say is most critical and urgent, think of what is most important to you, what most inspires you, and what motivates you to get involved.

Educate Yourself
Once you have pinpointed some philanthropic areas that motivate you to action, spend time researching them. What is currently being done? What needs to be done? What organizations are on the forefront and what are the different ways you can get involved?

Be Innovative

There are many organizations and community groups doing invaluable philanthropic work in many areas that need your support. However, sometimes there may not be an existing entity that is addressing the problems you think are important. In my case, there wasn't a nonprofit organization focused on the issues surrounding marriage and divorce that I found important, so I started my own. Look carefully for organizations that align with your vision, but don't be afraid to be innovative and create something new.

Get Involved

Money is an important component of most philanthropic efforts, but it is much more rewarding to give more than just cash. Supplement financial donations with the gift of your time, ideas, or contacts. Getting involved helps keep you educated and increases that feeling of progress and the knowledge that you are really making a difference.

Be Humble, But Loud

No one wants to be that person accused of being charitable just to get attention. The reward of philanthropy isn't recognition, it is the empowerment of using your voice and your resources to create change. While it is noble to be humble, it is also important to share your philanthropic experiences with your friends and your community to encourage them to identify their passions and get involved in the causes important to them.

It doesn't matter how much money you have to contribute. It doesn't matter whether you have a great deal of time to volunteer or just a few hours a month. It doesn't matter if you are 35, 54, or 68. It's never too late to create a vision for helping others and promoting positive changes. Take time to look at the world around you and choose the specific areas where you want to make a difference; it's such an empowering and fulfilling endeavor. Focusing your voice and your resources on the things that are most important to you lets you feel firsthand the power of your actions and thrive in a sense of accomplishment and purpose.

Section Seven

HAVING FUN
LIKE A GROWN-UP

36

Get your mojo working

The only thing better than having more sex is having more good sex. Yes, it *does* get better with age.

BY MARC C. GITTELMAN, M.D.

Marc Gittelman, M.D., completed his surgical and urology training in New York City at the Mount Sinai Medical Center. He is the founder and director of the Miami Center for Sexual Health, one of the first centers in the country to provide a fully integrated approach to sexual problems for both men and women. He also writes a regular column on sexual health for the *Miami Herald.*

A re you worried that your sex life might be going in the same direction as your face and thighs? If so, don't fret. I'm here to tell you that sex is like a fine wine — it should only improve with age. That's because sexual satisfaction is so closely linked to emotional and partner satisfaction. And we know from the medical literature that satisfaction within a relationship tends to increase over time.

So how can you continue to make your sex life as thrilling as you remember it from your 20s? Or, if you are one of the lucky couples who still have "steamy" romantic interludes, maybe you're asking: How can I make sure the hot sexual temperature of my relationship doesn't fade?

The answer is the same: We need to understand and overcome some of the obstacles we encounter as we age, including the physical and hormonal changes our bodies inevitably undergo. Just as important, you need to face the challenge of keeping the intimacy and passion in your relationship new and fresh, regardless of how many years you've been together.

I'm going to start with the male side of the equation: With the arrival of Viagra in 1999, the phrase "erectile dysfunction" was everywhere. Viagra and the two drugs that followed, Cialis and Levitra, addressed a fairly simple concept: As men age, the blood supply to all their organs — including the sexual organs — decreases.

Throw medical problems like diabetes, high blood pressure, obesity, and the use of certain medications into the mix, and it's no wonder that by age 50, nine out of 10 men have had at least one of "those" times.

Today, more than 30 million men have used at least one of the three available drugs that can resolve erection problems in more than 80 percent of men. Knowing that having and maintaining an erection won't be a problem brings a renewal of shared intimacy and lovemaking — and a stronger relationship. So don't be afraid to talk to your doctor about your sex life.

Then it's time to figure out how to get your partner as interested as you are. A well-respected study on sexuality from the University of Chicago found that 67 percent of women say they think about sex a few times a week or a few times a month. Compare that to 54 percent of men, who think about sex at least once a day, often several times a day. It gives new meaning to the phrase "sexual differences."

That survey also found that while men are mostly interested in sex, women want romance and love. Nearly eight out of 10 women said they enjoyed the caressing and hugging before intercourse far more than sex itself. And men? Well, nearly the same percentage said they viewed foreplay as nothing more than a necessary prelude to sex.

Take this dichotomy and add in declining hormone levels, physical changes, and the dual or triple roles most middle-aged women play today, and it's no wonder researchers find that nearly 35 percent of women say they have a low sex drive.

While there is a new specialty devoted to treating female sexual dysfunction, which uses a team approach to treat women who have problems with desire, arousal, or orgasm, unfortunately, the medical treatment side of things for women lags far behind that for men. But potential treatments are in the research pipeline, including a testosterone patch that may help replace low levels of a woman's testosterone (which plays a major role in her sex drive, just as it does in a man's).

But all the pills and patches in the world won't improve your sex life if your mind isn't into it. Here is my three-step plan to revitalize your sex life:

1. Revive the emotional components of your relationship. Take romantic vacations, plan surprise dinners of caviar and champagne, sign up for tango lessons. While spontaneity is great, the most effective way to integrate romance into your life is to have a planned "date." Planned sex can, and should be, a part of these dates.

2. Be a better "soul mate."

For the men, this means:
- Listening to her. Turn the television off, put the newspaper down, and look at her while she's talking.
- Appreciating her work demands/home demands/ child demands and making an effort to be part of

her team, not just a "helper."

• Telling her how much you really love her and then showing her with hand-holding, sensual and nonsensual touching, and gift-giving.

For the women, this means:

• Learning how to "play" with your partner. Consider taking an active part in or at least pretending to be interested in sports or other activities he would love to share with you.

• Pulling out the silky lingerie.

• Entertaining his fun sexual fantasies (and making sure he entertains yours).

• Telling him that he is the "greatest" lover. Eventually, he will be.

3. Enhance your own sensuality. You need to reawaken your senses to see, feel, listen to, and touch the person in front of you as though you were seeing, feeling, and touching him or her for the very first time. Part of this is mindset, and there are several games or exercises that work very, very well.

• Pretend this is your first date. Look at one another as if this were the first time you were seeing and smelling each other. Flirt. And when it feels right, make the kiss as special and slow and romantic as that very first kiss was.

• Show your partner the areas of your body that you want touched. I teach lovers to use red and green sticky dots, putting the green (for "go") dots on hot and ready spots, and the red (for "stop") dots on the prohibited or cautious zones. Maybe even a few yellow ones for "go slow." You and your lover are sure to have a few fun surprises along the way.

When all is said and done, sexuality is about achieving a meld of body, mind, and soul with your lover. In your 20s, this was often driven by your body's response to raging hormones. By the time you reach 50, you've reached a time for rediscovering your lover.

With this maturity, your body can enjoy sexual intimacy at a level of total and complete satisfaction that would have been impossible to achieve when you were younger. ☀

37

Drive a race car

Admit it: You're dying to try something dirty, noisy, uncomfortable, expensive, exhausting, frightening, exhilarating, terrifying, and downright dangerous.

BY ED MCCABE

An adventurer and author as well as a successful advertising man, Ed McCabe was the first American to drive the grueling Paris/Dakar Rally. His book about that experience, *Against Gravity*, was published by Warner Books. He has written on both business and adventure for *The New York Times, Playboy, Esquire, The Automobile, New York Magazine,* and other publications.

F ew things you can do in life are as dirty, noisy, uncomfortable, expensive, exhausting, frightening, exhilarating, terrifying, and downright dangerous as driving a race car. In fact, can you think of any other endeavor that can even lay claim to as many diverse adjectives? What other pastime offers up so many obvious and persuasive reasons for not doing it? But strapping yourself into a 300-horsepower racing machine and popping the clutch might be the best way to break through the age 50 barrier.

Having done it, I can tell you this: Nothing you will ever attempt (nothing legal anyhow) will give you the same rapturous feeling of having gotten away with something.

But that's just the slightly twisted and quirky explanation for what motivates a human to travel so fast on land that the field of vision becomes narrowed by half while color perception evaporates into a dreamlike state, where only the gray shred of a colorless thread separates life from possible death.

Note to women: Race car driving tends to be a man's sport, though I know more female racing drivers than female football players. The motivation for women to drive race cars will likely be at least a little different from that of men, who indeed most likely exhibited this inclination at the age of three when pushing a ketchup bottle across the kitchen floor, going "vroom-vroom!"

The fact is, people of different sexes, ages, and sizes drive racing cars. Anyone with some innate craziness, however infinitesimal, and the desire, determination, and money to do it, can do it. The latter is the only requirement that keeps the sport from being wholly democratic.

Once you had to drive fast in unacceptable and unexpected places to practice this calling. Now you can buy a car and show up somewhere at a race. Doesn't matter what kind of car. Win. Then it's got you like nothing will ever get you.

Part of you loves it, part of you hates it, but inescapably now, all of you, in every pore and breath and circumstance, needs it. Until you've tasted victory, you'll never understand the disgusting smell of defeat. You need that element of competitiveness in you.

I know a 40-ish mother of three who started racing because it was something she could share with her husband that wasn't golf. Now she loves it because it helps her forget her husband and her family. She says that she also likes being better than the person in the next car.

Another racing friend likes racing because of the feeling it gives him in his ass. As if it's physically on the line and he can feel completely the margin of danger and safety he's traveling on. Maybe that's the ultimate feeling of control. But he also likes learning. Knows that that's what racing is: the search for a faster line through a turn, the ever deeper dives into corners before braking, the squirrelly feeling of the car edging around disaster. That ass feel.

He likes the camaraderie. The sharing of a uniquely individual experience others share generically, lost as they are in their own individuality. That's a club.

If you haven't done it before, you can try it without commitment; just try to be as good as you can be in that moment. There are racing driver's schools all over the United States, Canada, Europe, and Australia. You can find one just about anywhere you're likely to find yourself.

But if you think you have the itch, you'd better scratch it soon. Fifty is about the age most people start thinking of preserving what's left of their existence rather than squandering it. Sure, Paul Newman was driving competitively at 80. But he started young, at 40.

There are schools for learning to drive competitively almost any kind of car you ever dreamed of driving. From four-wheel drives to go-karts to sleek sports-racing cars to open-wheel formula cars to NASCAR-type stock cars. Name your poison. Sign up. Learn. Even if you don't have the craziness to go on to compete and win, you'll gain a lot from the experience.

Give yourself a day on the wet skid pad pulling G's, controlling a near-uncontrollable car with the throttle alone. Get out on the track and put your foot to the floor and your heart into your mouth.

You'll learn the true meaning of getting your priorities straight. There's no time for thinking, only for doing right and not doing wrong. All else is superfluous.

Great training for the rest of your life.

38

Play golf in Scotland

Nothing will spark — or even rekindle — your love for the game like a trip to the land where golf began.

BY BILL DANIELS

Bill Daniels is the founder and CEO of the Golf Chicago Group, a multimedia communications, publishing, and consulting company. He first went to Scotland in 1992. He also is on the Board of The First Tee of North Chicago, and in July 2004 played 90 holes of golf in one day, walking and carrying his bag while raising nearly $10,000 in pledged donations for The First Tee.

Fifty is a great age to fall in love with golf. And it's the perfect time for you to rekindle the passion for golf you might have had at an earlier age. And if that passion has not died, if it is still burning with a white heat, what I am about to suggest to you post-50 golfers will only deepen your commitment to this marvelous lifelong game. In fact, do these three things and I guarantee that the game of golf will sustain and satisfy you for the next two or three decades — easily!

First, pay a visit to legendary Scotland, golf's historic birthplace. It was there that golf began, and all those who consider themselves complete golfers should seize the opportunity to play the country's windswept links and the highland's hidden gems (as for those of you who are shaking your heads saying, "Been there, done that" — just hang on. I've got something for you, too).

Golf in Scotland is more than just a game; it is part of the Scottish way of life, as integral to its society as firecrackers are to our Fourth of July celebrations. The Scots instinctively appreciate the deepest mysteries that the game holds, not to mention the insistent grip it can have on the soul.

Playing in Scotland also will introduce you to some of the strangest, funkiest golf holes and courses you have ever experienced. By most American standards, you could call much of Scottish golf "extreme golf." Blind shots, stone walls around greens, vertical-walled bunkers — it's all there. But once you understand that Scottish golf is all about life, it begins to make sense.

Just as life is (all too often) a rather untidy — and even unfair — game, so too is golf in Scotland. The deeper you get into Scottish golf, the easier it is to acknowledge that those funky bounces, good or bad, and those "unfair" lies are all merely parts of the game. At some point, you may even come to smile at the unexpected twists and turns the game can take (again, just like in life). In short, golf in Scotland is simply a wonderful elixir for the mind and the soul. You can't come away from it without gaining some greater understanding of what "it" is all about. Whatever "it" is.

On more practical terms, there are two ways that golfers "do" Scotland. The first is to use one of the many booking agencies that specialize in overseas golf holidays. They don't necessarily come cheap, so shop around and get references.

The second method is arguably more fun, whether you're a Scotland rookie or a seasoned veteran: to go solo, or with a spouse, a friend, or a partner as a twosome, with little or no reserved tee times or booked hotels. I wholeheartedly recommend this for anyone who has already experienced Scotland via the first approach. You were coddled well enough then; now, going it on your own will deepen your education in the land where it all began. Full disclosure: My own very first golf excursion to Scotland was solo, with only one secured tee time and one hotel reservation . . . and it was a most excellent adventure.

There are plenty of wonderful books about getting around Scotland and its courses, but the standout is *Golf in Scotland* by American Allan Ferguson (www.fergusongolf.com), which will give you all the help you need. One word of advice, though, which I learned the hard way: Double the estimated driving time, or at least add 50 percent. Trust me on this.

Second on my list of things to do after you turn 50 is to give back to golf. I'm going to assume that over the years, golf has given you a great deal, whether in friendship, memorable moments of beauty or excitement, or feelings of exultation. So shouldn't there be some obligation to give back something of ourselves?

Of course, you can always make a donation to your favorite golf charity, but I have another idea: Think about junior golf. First, by encouraging kids to learn golf, you are promoting the growth of our beloved game and introducing them to a pastime that will give pleasure for the rest of their lives. The second reason is that it's a sure way to recapture the simple joy of the game. There are few things as gratifying as the delight that lights up a kid's face after he or she stripes that first "perfect shot" down the fairway.

If you are looking for a program to support, call your local park district, YMCA, or check out The First Tee (www.TheFirstTee.com), a national organization that helps introduce golf to youngsters of all backgrounds. While The First Tee teaches golf, its true mission is to help develop character and good old life-enhancing values of honesty, integrity, and sportsmanship. There are more than 150 First Tee chapters in the United States — one is likely close to you.

Finally, for those of us passing the big 5-0 who just want to know: Is there anything we can do at this point to improve our own golf game? Of course, there may be a few golfers out there who are perfectly pleased with the state of their game, but most of us, I believe, at least occasionally wonder, "What if?"

If this sounds familiar, start by asking how *committed* you are to improving your game past 50. Don't be too quick to answer, either, because improvement doesn't come easily at any age. But it can be accomplished. The answer is simple and it has always been out there: lessons. (What? You thought I was going to say a new driver? Get real.) I'm talking lessons from a PGA professional. Not from a magazine. Not from your uncle Harry who once broke 80.

Yes, the solution is lessons, and that means plural. If you do commit, the emphasis has to be on real change, not short-term gimmicks. I believe that a golfer must commit to at least a full season of lessons in order to see real improvement. The good news is that today's PGA professional is better schooled in the fundamentals of the modern golf swing. For those of us who learned golf in the 1960s, this may mean some clear changes.

But don't be alarmed; if you are an astute golfer, you very well may become fascinated with the process as your understanding of the swing deepens. So get out there and enjoy — some of your best golf experiences are still ahead. ☼

39

Throw a slow-dance party

**Marvin Gaye. Smokey Robinson. Frank Sinatra.
Invite a crowd of 50-somethings in to hear the sexiest
music ever, and feel the room heat up.**

BY NELSON GEORGE

Writer, filmmaker, and cultural critic, Nelson George was
black-music editor of *Billboard* for seven years as well as
a *Village Voice* columnist. He is the author of 10 books,
fiction and nonfiction, including *Where Did Our Love Go:
The Rise and Fall of the Motown Sound.* His short film, *To Be
a Black Man,* featuring Samuel L. Jackson, has played in
film festivals around the world, as has his documentary,
A Great Day in Hip Hop.

O n Valentine's Day, I decided to host a party. Not
a sweaty, up-tempo dominated throw down, but
a gathering fueled by the musical sensibilities of
my youth. I decided to a give an old-school, red-light-
in-the-basement slow-jam party. Initially it was a selfish
notion. I've spent much of my life writing about popular

music but, as my favorite artists either died or faltered, I craved the opportunity to hear this music through high-quality speakers at a cool club.

I didn't realize how much the tradition of touch dancing and intimacy was a generational tradition until I started talking about the event. The idea elicited squeals of delight from adult women. From grown men it drew relieved smiles — finally, a party they could attend and not look like the white guy from the Will Smith romantic comedy *Hitch*. Married couples saw it as an occasion to relive memories of passion long forgotten amidst stampeding kids and stacks of bills. From young singles, I sensed a satisfaction that they, finally, were being welcomed into the secret society of adulthood. I called it a Grown Folks party and, for all the attendees, that, as much as the music, was the attraction. Boomers, often portrayed as overgrown adolescents, found in this idea an acceptance of adulthood on their own terms.

The art of the slow jam, as practiced by masters such as Marvin Gaye, Smokey Robinson, and Frank Sinatra (you haven't lived until a DJ has mixed "Summer Wind" into "You Really Got a Hold On Me") suggest a lost world where you can still smoke in clubs, heads resting on shoulders and the warmth of two bodies becoming familiar. For those pushing or just pushed past fifty, this was a very familiar space. We didn't just dance this way at proms. The slow dance was a coming-of-age ritual for a great many Boomers, one fraught with anxiety, surprise, and opportunity. Who among us, except the most exceptional looking, have not felt the fear that no one will want to dance with us? And how great was the joy when someone did? And, finally, do you recall the wonder when you actually rocked in the same rhythm?

Growing up in New York, a city known for its sexuality, more than its sensuality, I lived in an area where basement parties were a weekly event. Moreover, there was always time for slow dancing or grinding, a kind of vertical foreplay that I recall with great affection. But slow dancing was never just a black or urban thing. Down South, fans of country as well as soul and pop were always at it.

There are a lot of things that define the Baby Boomer's relationship to popular music: the massive stadium concert, overt (and covert) political commentary, the concept of concept albums, AM top-40 radio, the transition from analog to digital, and the steady sexualizing of lyrics. There is a tendency to look at the Boomer's relationship to music only through the prism of rock's excess: LSD, Woodstock, indulgent guitar solos, unkempt jeans, couples wiggling to music several feet away from each other. From this point of view, all of us around 50 were hippies who later sold our souls for yuppie comforts. It is a convenient myth that both left-wing nostalgia merchants and right-wing pundits exploit to their advantage. But if you really look at the sweep of our musical experience, it's clear that this stereotype represents just one aspect of ourselves.

As much as we were part of a radical musical movement, we also harbored an intense romanticism. This yearning for emotional connection, fired by the challenges of war and social change, as well as our own personal journeys, runs through the work of the era's best-loved artists. When you consider the work of Sam Cooke, the Beatles, the Beach Boys, Bob Dylan, Smokey Robinson, Aretha Franklin, Carole King, Stevie Wonder, the Eagles, Joni Mitchell, Willie Nelson, Bob Marley, Barry White, Paul Simon, the Bee Gees, and so many others, that desire to understand and express love is undeniable. Whether we categorize the music as soul, country rock, reggae, singer-songwriter, or disco, there is a common thread that unites them. And it is that shared sensibility that has produced the verses we hum, the choruses we sing, and the way we move our hips. Long after we stopped playing air guitar to Led Zep's "Whole Lotta Love," we still sing along in our car to Paul McCartney's "My Love" and Gaye's "Distant Lover."

At the slow-jam party, people reacted with shouts when "Let's Get It On" came on; they slid closer when we surprised them with "Lay, Lady, Lay;" and they looked into each other's eyes and swayed to "Let's Stay Together." The intros to songs, just a bass intro or a drum downbeat or a familiar voice singing a well-remembered opening line, produced murmurs. People got up out of their seats and pressed close. They weren't moved by this music simply out of nostalgia. They embraced it (and each other) because it's music that still speaks to an inarticulate yearning for a multi-leveled emotional connection, also known as love. At 50, we still feel the power of these songs to raise temperatures. In fact, watching the adult crowd dance slowly, some mouthing the words in their lover's ears, I could see that time has given this music more resonance, not less. All we need is love. Indeed. ☼

40

Lose the list

The best way to be a tourist is to trash your list and dive right in.

BY PETER GREENBERG

Peter Greenberg is America's most recognized, honored, and respected front-line travel news journalist. He is travel editor for CBS News, appearing on The Early Show *and across many CBS broadcast platforms. His books include the* New York Times *best-seller* Don't Go There! The Travel Detective's Essential Guide to the Must-Miss Places of the World, *and many others. For more information, visit www.PeterGreenberg.com.*

Turning 50 means it is time — if you haven't done so already — to jettison "the list." Now, don't deny you have one. We are a nation of list makers, especially when it comes to travel.

A destination is either on your list, or it's not. And experience dictates that the list itself is ridiculous and misleading — literally. "I don't want to go there . . . it's not on my list." Not on your "list"? Let's start by what most people have on their list: Western Europe. Why?

It's almost as if there's an entire generation of failed art history majors out there who desperately need to see Florence . . . at least once . . . so they can check it off their list.

Dump the list. It's only something to depart from. And if you insist on having a list, then the list must include every place you *haven't* been, every experience you *haven't* had. And then look at that list only once and repeat after me: I will not SHOULD on myself.

By the time I turned 50, travel had become synonymous with breathing. It's an involuntary act and, like inhaling and exhaling, I travel to stay alive.

I don't plan to travel. I just travel, because I firmly believe that a plan, like that list, is only something to depart from. And therein lies the real beauty of travel — the idea, the opportunity, and the manifestation of being spontaneous without being irresponsible. Not only to think, but to live — literally — outside the box. And the key to the true serendipity of travel is to remove the word "later" from your vocabulary. Every time you use "later" in a sentence, you either don't do it as well . . . or worse, you don't do it at all.

My father once told me that the key to life is not being smart or beautiful or right or rich. The key, he explained, is in how you adjust to what life gives you. Any kind of travel challenges you to adjust. It's how well you adjust, how fast you adjust, and how sensitively you adjust that makes the difference.

There has been a sea of change in the way people approach travel. It's no longer about the affordability of the destination. Instead, it's about the accessibility of the experience.

I was visiting Shanghai by cruise ship in 1984. As I walked along the pier, heading toward a planned group bus tour of the city, a distinguished-looking, well-dressed Chinese man who looked to be in his early 40s rode up to me on his bicycle. "You from the ship?" he asked in perfect English. "Yes," I replied, asking, "Do you live here?" He smiled. "All my life!" When I remarked about his mastery of English, he startled me. "Actually," he said, "this is really the first time I've been able to speak it since . . . 1949." I never got on the bus. A few minutes later, 78-year-old Joe Cheng was taking me on one of the more remarkable journeys of my life — the history of Shanghai through his eyes.

A few years later, I was touring one of the Philippine islands when we pulled into a hotel driveway. There, parked along the side, were 10 motorcycles. I asked who owned the bikes. One of the bellmen said he was a medical student, and the other medical students in Legaspi had formed a motorcycle club. I asked if I could rent one of the motorcycles. "I've got a better idea," he said. "Would you like for me to round up the other club members and take you for a bike tour?" An hour later, nine motorcyclists — plus me — were headed through a half dozen villages and toward an active volcano, a tour I'll never forget.

About 10 years ago, as I was leaving a Manhattan hotel, terribly late for the airport, I jumped into a yellow cab. "JFK," I ordered, along with directions, "head up Madison Avenue, turn right on 96th street, if the East River Drive is too crowded, then head up Third Avenue instead..."

The driver simply said in a thick Middle Eastern accent . . . , "No, I'll take you a better way." A better way? Already stressed because I was so late, I was ready for a fight, or at least an argument. "Hey pal," I shot back. "I'm from New York. Just take me the way I want to go." But he was ready to take me that better way. "Let me ask you," he began. "What terminal do you want?" I told him Terminal Nine. "OK, we take my way, and if you're not at Kennedy in 26 minutes, the ride is free." Deal. The driver then took me on a route I had never been on in my life. And, shockingly, 22 minutes later, I arrived at JFK. The driver smiled. "You owe me," he, said laughing.

I asked his name. William. Where was he from? Alexandria, Egypt. But he lived in New Jersey. Was this his own cab? Yes. Then I had an idea. I took down his phone number and his cab number. And for the next eight years, William Megalla was my driver every time I came to New York. He drove my friends. He drove for my mother.

One day, while driving me into the city from the airport, he said he wanted to tell me some good news. His younger brother, Billy, was getting married, and his family wanted to invite me to the wedding. Would I go? Of course. Two months later, I was at that wedding . . . in Alexandria, Egypt. And that trip taught me a valuable lesson. In New York, William was just a cab driver. In Egypt, he was a god. The wedding took place at 10 p.m. inside King Farouk's palace on the Mediterranean. Five hundred celebrating Egyptian Coptics, and a guy named Greenberg.

So what are your new rules, now that you're turning 50? Spontaneity without being irresponsible. Going with the flow. Forgetting brochures. But never forgetting common sense.

Of course there is always the ticking clock as you get older. But travel after 50 slows that clock down as you speed up — it allows you to immerse yourself in a world of endless possibilities, a world where the debilitating borders of fear and misunderstanding become increasingly easy to ignore and, thankfully, a world where you can firmly embrace the notion that travel is a powerful force to build bridges, where every ride to the airport may not just be a short-term means to an end, but the start of a lifelong friendship. ☼

41

Go fishing

Some might say that 50 is too old to start fishing. Not so. It's never too late . . . and when you fish, you'll discover a lot more than what is at the end of your line.

BY JAMES PROSEK

Called "the Audubon of the Fishing World" by *The New York Times*, James Prosek is an artist and author who lives in Easton, Connecticut, and has been featured in such publications as *People, Sports Illustrated, Sports Afield,* and *Life.* His book, *The Complete Angler,* was turned into an ESPN special, which won the Peabody Award.

Some might say that 50 is too old to start fishing. That is not so. If you have reached your 50s and have not yet exercised your primal instincts, then you have an exciting adventure in store, and I believe that fishing will also offer you an opportunity to be more at peace with yourself and with the world.

I once wrote several years ago that the *Compleat Angler*, Izaak Walton's seminal work of 1653 on fishing as a contemplative recreation, "is not about fishing, it's about life. Or rather, it is about fishing, but fishing is life." I would like to qualify that. One of the reasons that "fishing is life" is because it is part of our fabric. The act of stalking and capturing a fish, I'd like to think, is part of our development as cognitive beings. We are, after all — much as we try in day-to-day life to shake millions of years of evolution — hunter-gatherers.

There is evidence that Walton himself did not start fishing until he was 40. He may be the single most influential fisherman who ever lived because his book was the first to outline the idea of predation as a recreation for contemplation. He adopted fishing into his life and found that many life lessons could be communicated metaphorically using fishing as the vehicle. The *Compleat Angler* is instructional, a dialogue between a fisherman and a hunter where the fisherman ends up converting the hunter to his passion. A favorite passage in the book occurs when the hunter's line breaks on a big trout, and he says, "My rod is broken and I lost the fish." The fisherman then corrects him. "Nay, the trout is not lost, for you cannot lose what you never had." If you have the time and the patience, angler or not, I would recommend reading Walton's book.

As a young boy, without any instruction, I became obsessed with creatures in the pond on our dead-end street. When my friend Stephen gave me a fishing rod at the age of nine, I was given my freedom. My mother had just left home, and fishing became the only activity that made me feel secure and happy in a time when things were anything but certain. Why did it feel so natural? Perhaps the hunter (and by this I don't mean bloodthirsty killer) within me had just been waiting for an opportunity to emerge.

Though modern angling is more for recreation than survival, the activity keeps our primal instincts fresh and alert. Many anglers today, including myself, practice catch and release. It may seem counter-intuitive to describe anglers as predatory if they let the fish go, but killing was never the only facet of predation. As hunters, we evolved with an admiration for our prey that made us more acute observers, which in turn made us better survivors. The earliest known drawings on cave walls were of animals that hunters were pursuing, an expression of that admiration that evolved in the throes of strategy and pursuit. Angling, perhaps, is a form of predation that plays up the aspect of admiration more than the goal of killing.

Izaak Walton called angling "a gentle art" — a phrase that does not bring to mind whacking things on the head, gutting them, and eating them. Though Walton ate fish, he had the sensibility and the admiration for the prey that a catch-and-release fisherman does. To Walton, angling was spiritual. The author notes that the first followers of Christ, the apostles, were fishermen; humble observant men who followed peace. They were "fishers of men." Spirituality of some sort is an undeniable aspect of modern-day fly-fishing. When you are out in nature, by the stream, you can lose all sense of time and space and become one with the river. The river is essentially an immortal eternity, always flowing, even while we remain mortal. So it's nice to look down and see our reflection in eternity.

If you have never angled, a good initial approach is through books. Other great angling works that convey the spirituality of the pastime are *A River Runs Through It* by Norman Maclean, *The River Why* by James David Duncan, and a small personal favorite of mine, *The Year of the Trout* by David M. Carroll. Reading any one of these stories will get you hooked and once you get into fishing, it is hard to get out of it.

For a beginner fly fisherman, I recommend starting with trout fishing. Get a pair of chest-high waders, a nine-foot-long, five-weight fly rod, a reel with five-weight line, a box of assorted flies, a pair of polarized sunglasses for cutting down glare on the water, as well as providing eye protection, and if you can afford it, a guide to take you out.

You can learn a great deal from someone who knows how to fish. If you don't have the patience to learn how to cast a fly from reading books, watching videos, and experimenting, you can always find an instructor. Orvis Flyfishing Schools (www.orvis.com) have programs nationwide to teach you how to fish.

One of the greatest things about fishing is the places that it can take you. Once fishing is in your blood and you're ready to travel, I recommend a trip to one of two places: Alaska or New Zealand. You won't forget it, and you'll carry it with you the rest of your life. The author Robert Traver once wrote, "Trout will not, indeed, cannot live, except where beauty dwells." I've found that to be pretty much true, having chased trout from Connecticut to California, France to Mongolia. Wild trout require cool clean water to survive, so you usually find them in pristine wilderness settings.

Fishing is a sport you can do at home or abroad, alone or with friends, anywhere there is water — and you'll discover so much more than what is at the end of your line. ☼

42

Check your "turning 50" horoscope

Yep, it's still the Age of Aquarius: Now that you've hit the big 5-0, here's what to expect.

BY KAT LANE

Professional astrologer Kat Lane writes horoscopes and astrological features for numerous publications including *Marie Claire, Mademoiselle,* and *In Style.* Lane's stellar insights are featured online at Swoon, Conde Nast's popular website where her interactive Love Matches continue to be the site's most "clicked-on" feature. She is a member of the National Council for Geocosmic Research and has served on the organization's board of directors.

T hink of the planets as celestial guides that help light our paths along a journey of self-discovery. Before there were metroplexes and plasma TVs to divert our attention, the ancients pulled up a rock and watched real stars perform in the night sky. Over time, they began to notice a correlation between the movements in the heavens and our actions on earth. As above, so below. By putting us in sync with the natural rhythms and cycles of the universe, the study of astrology can help us plan our lives more effectively. The stars can't force you to go anywhere; they can only point the way. Planning a move? Your retirement? The levitation of the Pentagon? Why not check out your cosmic map? Timing is everything. See what the stars have in store now that you've crossed the threshold into the fabulous 50s.

ARIES (3/21–4/20)

You've never looked — let alone acted — your age, and there's no reason to start now. And if you're like most rams, you're still loaded with brio and eager as ever to take on new challenges. Here's one to test your mettle: Try completing just a few of the millions of projects you've started. You were blessed with great initiative, but you've always lacked follow-through. So while you're still able to travel in the fast lane, why not try crossing some "finish" lines?

TAURUS (4/21–5/20)

"I have, therefore I am" is the Taurean credo. If you are a typical "material bull," hitting your 50s may come as a shock when suddenly the "beemer" ain't beamin', the Cristal's lost its fizz, and the Armani doesn't seem to fit. When those creature comforts no longer satisfy, you need to think about tempering your raw materialism and tuning in to a higher plane. I'm not saying you have to turn into Shirley MacLaine and go out on a cosmic limb (although she *is* a Taurus), but it is time to discover the sacred cow within.

GEMINI (5/21–6/20)
Welcome to your 50s! In addition to getting your AARP card, you're now eligible to enroll in "The Big Picture," an exciting course that allows you to cultivate a global perspective and ponder new philosophies. Because you've perceived life in all its dizzying detail, you've never seen the forest for the trees (so many leaves, so little time). I think you'll find that adding this wide-angle view to your current perspective will prove both exciting and meaningful.

CANCER (6/21–7/22)
Come out, come out, wherever you are! The universe is prompting you soft-shelled crabs to vacate your safe havens and explore new terrain. The I-never-leave-my-zip-code types among you will find this terrifying. No one is asking you to go claw to claw with a wild beast in Borneo. It's more likely you'll traverse the realms of the mind by, say, taking a philosophy course, exploring different religions and/or exotic cultures. The best part for you homebodies? You have all of your 50s to accomplish this and you never have to leave your neighborhood.

LEO (7/23–8/22)

Remember how Superman could transform a lump of coal into a diamond by squeezing it in his fist? Now that you're 50, the cosmos is exerting similar pressure on you to do what you sun gods were meant to do: Shine. If you've been coasting on your charisma, it's time to test your talent. You're ready to roar! I know you egoists will have no problem reflecting on your brilliance. You'll know you're making progress if you can do it without a mirror.

VIRGO (8/23–9/22)

You germ-phobes have a nasty reputation for disinfecting everything (and everyone) in sight. Why not turn this urge to purge on yourself and break free of these restricting stereotypes? Now that you've reached 50, the cosmos is granting you permission to stop mopping up everyone else's messes. If you do, you'll no longer be married to the miniscule, the menial, and the mundane. Stop acting like Felix Unger on steroids: You can reach for the stars and become the legend you were meant to be.

LIBRA (9/23–10/22)

It's a cosmic paradox that you, the sign of equality and justness, so often sacrifice your own needs for peace-at-all-costs. The problem, my fair Libra, is not that you put the desires of others ahead of your own, but *instead* of your own. How "fair" is that? Now that you're 50, the cosmos is cajoling you to drop the people-pleasing mask and the need to keep up appearances. Unleash your inner warrior! Let down your hair, pick up the sword and fight for *your* right to party! You must do this to fulfill your astrological destiny. It's called balance.

SCORPIO (10/23–11/21)

The skeptic in you scoffs that I dare profess to know what you'll do in your 50s. You're right, I don't. All I can tell you is what energies are activating your chart and when. How, and with whom, you choose to manifest them is between you and your free will. That said, my hunch is you're going to become a lot more trusting and willing to purge yourself of old hang-ups, neuroses, and obsessions. And in the *very* near future you'll be radiating more faith, hope, and cock-eyed optimism than a Sagittarius. It's already happening. You're reading this horoscope.

SAGITTARIUS (11/22–12/21)

You jet-setters are infamous for escaping to faraway places when things get too close for comfort. Seems the only baggage you're comfortable handling is carry-on. But scattering your attentions (and affections) keeps you from enjoying deeper experiences. Now that you're 50, the cosmos is exhorting you to explore some truly foreign territory — your feelings. Success here depends on your willingness to be profound and emotionally connected. In other words, acting as unlike yourself as possible. Finally, a challenge worthy of your adventurous nature!

CAPRICORN (12/22–1/19)

Life begins at 50 for you late-bloomers: You start out as old goats and end up as playful kids. Why? Because you were so overly responsible growing up. What other sign can boast that they put both parents through school with money from their paper routes? In recompense, the universe offers a second childhood just when you're smart enough to enjoy it. So explore your playful, creative side, kick up your heels, and act like a "kid" again. After all, there's more to life than work.

AQUARIUS (1/20–2/18)

Don't trust anyone over 30 was the rallying cry at the dawning of the Age of Aquarius. Even at 50, you mavericks can boast that you're still true to the spirit, if not the letter, of that sentiment. Here's your chance to prove it. The cosmos is challenging you to let go of some long-held, deeply entrenched ideals in order to realize a long-term goal. Now you can show the world how radical you truly are, because this time the "establishment" you're expected to overthrow is your own. So stay cool and remember: Don't trust anyone *under* 30!

PISCES (2/19–3/20)

Strange visitors from another planet, you sensitive souls came to earth with talents and abilities far beyond those of mere mortals. Sadly, earth's bleak realities often crush your spirit, forcing some of you to drown your sorrows in designer martinis rather than realizing your artistic potential. Knowing the unfair burden placed upon you, the cosmos sometimes intervenes by emboldening you to manifest your wildest dreams. Turning 50 is one such time. So instead of plucking olives from your glass, try plumbing the depths of your creativity. I guarantee it will be a lot more fruitful. ☀

43

Jump off a bridge

Every so often, it's good to defy your fears.

BY MARK FENTON

Mark Fenton hosts the PBS television series *America's Walking,* and is a consultant to the University of North Carolina's Pedestrian and Bicycle Information Center. He also serves as an instructor in the walkable community workshop series of the Washington D.C.-based National Center for Bicycling and Walking. He is the author of *The Complete Guide to Walking for Health, Weight Loss, and Fitness* (Lyons Press, 2001).

I t may not be the first idea you have when you turn 50, but I guarantee it will be the best: Go jump off a bridge.

I've come to the realization that most people don't jump off nearly enough bridges in their lifetimes. They stay on the safe side of the railing, doing comfortable things — things that will turn out exactly as they envisioned. But once you crest 50, it's absolutely time to take a little leap. Or maybe a big one.

I say this as a guy who has spent the bulk of his adult
life trying to convince people to do more walking. "Get
out and walk every day," I say. "It's good for you." Talk
about boring. Talk about predictable. Talk about staying on the bridge. Nothing thrilling or unknown about
walking.

Sure, walking is good for you — daily walking burns
calories and helps you maintain a healthy weight as it
tones your muscles, clears your head, and improves your
mood. The Surgeon General says just 30 minutes of
walking a day reduces your risk of chronic disease, and
research confirms that regular walkers live longer, more
independent lives. All great things, all great reasons to
walk every day. But not really pushing the envelope.

That's why I had to jump off a bridge. Jumping helped
me realize how right I've been all along about the walking. I can best explain it with a little story.

A few years ago, I found myself at something of a midlife crisis. I was leaving a job of many years at *Walking
Magazine,* beginning work on a new PBS television series
(about walking), and writing a book called T*he Complete
Guide to Walking.* Our children were growing up, and
my career was decidedly, well, pedestrian.

My wife, Lisa, was getting nervous. She figured it was
only a matter of time before I was gripped by the inevitable question: Gibson six-string or Harley Davidson?

So around my birthday in July, she took me out to our favorite local bistro to celebrate the person I had become. A person who talks about walking, eating your vegetables, and being healthy. I was appreciative, but unconvinced.

Returning to our neighborhood that evening, we crossed a bridge that forms a gentle arc over a tidal estuary — a small river whose flow shifts with the tide. Sometimes the water is deep and swiftly flowing, sometimes it is a shallow trickle. As in many a coastal town, it's a summer rite of passage for the local kids to jump off the bridge into the current. Of course, you've got to time the tide and depth right, or you can end up with your feet sliced by razor-sharp barnacles. Or worse.

Two young girls in swimsuits were standing along the rail of the bridge. As they faced the water, their arms gripped the railing tightly, and both looked nervous about jumping. I heard a teenage boy — not the epitome of human good judgment — shout from the water below, "Go ahead, jump. It's deep enough, c'mon, let's go."

Instead of shouting the standard "It's always funny until someone puts out an eye!" we looked at the kids. We looked at the tide. I looked at Lisa. She looked at me. I looked at her again. I said nothing, and then she said, "Okay, give me your wallet. Go on, just be careful."

257

So I handed her my wallet, pulled off my shirt and sandals, and scrambled over the rail. The girls were astonished, and the boy yelled up, "Hey mister, you jumpin'?" (Like I needed a "hey mister" on my birthday.) And we all did — we jumped safely, swam to the side, and were soon on our merry ways.

The incident was worth it just for the thrill of the jump and to see the looks on the kids' faces. But I've left the most important detail out of the story. How do you figure Lisa and I had traveled to dinner that evening? We'd walked, of course. We passed those girls on foot, moving maybe three miles an hour, not 30. We weren't separated from them by thousands of pounds of automotive steel and glass, but by just a foot or two.

And with that, I realized two very important things about the walking that I do and that I encourage others to do. First, it reminded me that living an active lifestyle is its own reward. I don't walk *just* to keep my weight down, my cholesterol in check, or my doctor off my back. I do it so when the chance comes to jump off a bridge, hike a new trail, or go mountain biking, I'll be young enough at heart and fit enough in body to actually do it!

It's as simple as this: Being a walker assures that you won't miss your own bridge-jumping chance when it comes. *Your* bridge may be hang gliding or it may be taking a walking tour in France, but you won't have to pass it up if you stay active and fit. Whatever your plunge, get out for a walk, every single day, and when the chance comes to jump off a bridge, jump. You never know where you'll land. But I guarantee it will be a better place. ☀

44

Never cease the mental fight

Being older gives you the advantage of a deeper perspective.

BY HAROLD BLOOM

Harold Bloom is Sterling Professor of Humanities at Yale University, Berg Professor of English at New York University, and a former professor at Harvard. He holds honorary degrees from the universities of Rome and Bologna. His more than 20 books include *Shakespeare: The Invention of the Human, How to Read and Why,* and *Where Shall Wisdom Be Found?*

First of all, from the vantage point of 75, 50 doesn't seem much different from 20. But, although the benefits of learning are limitless, time is not. I've been saying for years that the real reason one should read the canonical, the traditional, and better works, is that, finally, there is less and less time. As I get older, I seem to be busier than I was the year before.

In a sense, learning can be considered a race against the clock, because there will never be enough time even if you read all your life, as I have. But obviously, you can't do *nothing* but read your whole life. Schopenhauer, a great book man, warns against that, and Emerson, who also aspired to read everything, issued a warning. He said, rather beautifully, "Reading is for a scholar's idle hours."

A teacher of literature at 75 years old is rather like one of those big league baseball pitchers, particularly if the teacher has been, as I think it's fair for me to say I was, and I hope still am, of a certain power and proficiency. The rare pitchers like Mr. Randy Johnson and Mr. Roger Clemens continue to be power pitchers at what many people consider middle age. Most pitchers who are still pitching into their mid-40s and have done it well — and there are a few of them in the big leagues — have become pitchers of a very different kind.

In some ways, like the baseball pitchers, I've improved as a teacher. (Maybe not my temperament, but my energy level is certainly different.) I used to go into the classroom with fire and passion and so much expressionistic drive that I didn't really give the students an opportunity to answer my questions or hold discussions. Now I'm much more patient. My happiest moments in the classroom are now when a discussion develops among the students that the whole class participates in. I some-times sit, listening to the way it develops and grows. I don't think that would have happened back in the days when I was, as it were, too much of a power pitcher.

So no age is too old to learn. To read that which is most worth reading can take you down a profound path. I have students in my classes — "old dogs" of 50, 60, or even 70 years old — and I've seen them learn. But unless one has developed aesthetic and intellectual standards, and some sense of what is wise or not, then an ocean of information is not necessarily a good thing. The challenge is to know what to learn and how to learn it. To learn to cultivate the ability to judge the truth of information is a major factor. And if one doesn't read and remember the very best that has been written, then he or she will never learn how to think critically, because thinking depends upon memory, and without memory, one can't think.

There are books that, if one reads them through and gets to know them well enough, are a classroom in and of themselves. They offer pleasure, of course, the pleasure of insight, among others. Shelley defines the sublime, which means the highest kind of experience one can have in reading, as learning to give up easier pleasures for the more challenging ones. Obviously Proust is a more difficult pleasure than most of the reading one picks up today.

At one point in my book *Where Shall Wisdom Be Found?* I quote, with great joy, a marvelous remark of Montaigne, "Don't bother yourself with preparing to learn how to die. When the times comes, you'll know how to do it well enough."

There's a beautiful moment in a William Blake hymn, a sort of non-conformist hymn. It's the poem that ends with, "I shall not cease from Mental Fight." I guess "I will not cease from mental fight" is central to me.

Reading and learning prepare us for how to live, and that means living up to the very end. My own interpretation, which my friend Tony Kushner is kind enough to have said he picked up from me and used as the cornerstone of *Angels in America,* is a translation of the biblical Blessing (with a capital B) as being "more life." Reading, as I view it, is a great Blessing, and it will potentially give one more life.

Section Eight

WATCHING THE BIG PICTURE

45

Don't go off the deep end

It took leaving his wife, losing his job, and getting lymphoma to show this America's Cup sailor who — and what — really mattered to him.

BY GARY JOBSON

Gary Jobson is a world-class sailor, a television commentator, and an author based in Annapolis, Maryland. He is president of US SAILING, the National Governing Body of Sailing. Gary has authored 16 sailing books and is editor at large of *Sailing World* and *Cruising World* magazines. Jobson has been ESPN's sailing commentator since 1985. He won an A.C.E. (Award for Cable Excellence) for the 1987 America's Cup. In 1988 Jobson won an Emmy® for his production work on sailing at the Olympic Games in South Korea and he won an Emmy® for the 2006 Volvo Ocean Race on PBS. He has covered the Olympics five times for NBC. Gary Jobson has won four Southam Awards and one Telly Award. He has been inducted into the America's Cup Hall of Fame.

I laugh when people say 50 is just a number. It wasn't for me. Attaching the number 50 to my name felt like a major milestone. All at once I had a sense of accomplishment, a feeling of freedom, and a sudden license to do things never before contemplated. In a word, I went "nuts" at a time when my health was perfect, my family life secure, and my business thriving. It was easy to take it all for granted. Turning 50 made me feel entitled to change my universe.

There had been bigger birthday celebrations. My surprise 40th party attracted 200 friends, family members, and business associates from across the country. It was nice. During that decade I watched my kids grow up, my reputation in the world of sailing advance, and my net worth shift from substantial debt to significant assets.

With all this good fortune, the obvious question would be, Why change anything? But in the three years after I turned 50, my world did change, for the worse, at every level.

Perhaps it was because I was in a rut. Home life had become routine. My wife of 26 years, Janice, started a new career as a teacher. She was busy, had her own sense of independence, and still looked after three active daughters. The girls spent increasing amounts of time doing their own thing, so I too went off in my own direction. In 1999 alone, I wrote 50 articles and one book, gave 63 lectures, produced 25 television shows, attended 42 board meetings, traveled 250 days, and received the Nathanael G. Herreshoff Award, the highest honor in

American sailing, for my contributions to the sport. It was exhilarating!

Our tight family was shooting off in five very different directions. My eldest daughter, Kristi, was preparing to attend Harvard. Twins Ashleigh and Brooke excelled in their respective sports, water polo and lacrosse. So, after a low-key 50th birthday party, I took our busy family sailing in Maine and Canada for a month on a special chartered 56-foot sailing yacht. But I had the rumbling feeling my family didn't really want to be there. The cruise was ambitious, rarely stopping at a marina, and I became frustrated when the inevitable squabbles bubbled up. When it was over, everyone seemed relieved to return to their regular schedules. I left for Sydney, Australia, to cover the Olympic sailing competition for NBC. When I returned from the fast-paced Games, my wife and daughters were comfortably ensconced in their daily routines. I felt like a "$10 extra" in a movie, neither needed nor appreciated.

Looking at some old pictures triggered a trip down memory lane, and I began reminiscing about an old girlfriend with whom I had raced small sailboats and shared an on-and-off romance between the ages of 16 and 22. When we met again, although we clearly weren't 16 anymore, we spent hours recalling our shared past. That led to more meetings, and we eventually left our respective families to be together. She, too, had just turned 50.

The next two years were a dizzying whirl of travel, television shows, speaking engagements, sailing, and the excitement of a new life. But deep down I didn't feel good about it. The slow divorce and the pain I was causing ripped me apart. The thrill of the new began to wane.

Then without warning, ESPN, my most important client of 16 years, decided to stop covering sailing, disastrous for me both financially and emotionally. My star began to fade. Or so I thought. The last major event we covered on ESPN was the 2003 America's Cup. We had the best coverage of the worst sporting event. After the American boats were eliminated early, the American public didn't care. Plus, the host New Zealand race officials kept delaying the race for days, waiting for favorable wind (for their team). The debacle understandably upset ESPN executives; the viewing audience abandoned the Cup in droves.

Leading up to the Cup I had gone a little loony. I stopped getting haircuts and got an earring. To my exceedingly polite friends, it must have looked like a massive midlife crisis.

In the midst of all this turmoil, I started to feel ill. I began coughing uncontrollably. At night, I woke up drenched from sweat. Red blotches appeared on my arms and legs. I lost a lot of weight, was chronically tired, and every night I vomited for hours. But I kept working. I set off on a 60-city lecture tour. It was hard. I was able to deliver the lectures, but everything else from travel to eating was difficult.

By my 23rd talk I could barely stand. A doctor in the audience said I didn't look good and invited me to his clinic the next morning. After five hours of tests, he said, "I don't know what's wrong with you, but you are very sick and need to go home." Just to be contrary, I gave presentations for three more nights before returning home to a little condo I had in Baltimore. It was lonely there. My old girlfriend visited infrequently. A sailing pal of mine who was a doctor arranged a series of tests that went on for 10 days, culminating — finally — in a diagnosis: lymphoma, cancer of the lymph nodes.

It took six rounds of chemo, surgery, high-dose chemo, a stem cell transplant, and 16 months before I was moving around comfortably.

Overwhelming worldwide support flooded in: e-mails, letters, visits. Janice, whom I had left, was there for me on a regular basis. Years before, she had been an oncology nurse and knew the challenges I faced.

I was constantly surprised by the many setbacks I experienced; it seemed for every two steps forward, there were more steps back.

After nearly a year of endless procedures, a stem cell transplant, and unbelievable pain, depression set in and I could feel myself slipping away. I couldn't walk. I was constantly drugged. But as I lay there, I thought: "I'm not done yet." I wasn't ready to check out. I felt an inner spark through all the confusion of drugs and pain, that I could still be constructive and productive. If I could get through this, I resolved to repair my marriage, work only on meaningful projects, embrace the kids' emerging independence, and savor good health.

It was a turn-around. During my darkest days, I wrote *Championship Sailing* with my longtime assistant, Kathy Lambert. Every day, chipping away at the book project, I was able to visualize my years of racing sailboats. Writing was good therapy and enabled me to chart a course that would get my health, and my life, back on track.

While sitting idle for months trying to get well, I calculated the total number of races I'd been in — about 5,000. There were so many rewards to this: the freedom spent on the water, sailing the waters off every continent, and seeing the world from this vantage point. Sailing was the vehicle that provided valuable lessons that sustained me through the most difficult period of my life.

I'm now halfway between 50 and 60. At the moment my cancer scans are clean. I'm living happily with Janice, our girls are off to college, and my business is back on track.

It's hard to know if stress can cause an illness, but I do know that we all make our own choices. Certainly, wind-shifts will come along the way. You can be on the water, with the wind at 10 mph and the sun out, and an hour later harsh conditions can strike, with the wind blowing 50 mph. In races I have usually been the tactician, the calm one who keeps things steady. You can't be in the middle of a race thinking about where you've been, you have to think about where you are now and where you want to go. You move on to the rest of the race. If you dwell on your mistakes, you'll never get back on track. Oddly, five years later and back on course, I have few regrets about my actions and circumstances.

My lesson is to savor what is good in life, adapt to change, and never give up trying to be better. With that attitude, you do move up in the fleet. For me, 50 is not just a number.

46

Let your life flash before your eyes

You're turning 50. Accept it, and make the experience worthwhile.

BY ROBERT THURMAN, PH.D.

Robert Thurman, Ph.D., is a scholar and the Jey Tsong Khapa Professor of Indo-Tibetan Buddhist Studies in the Department of Religion at Columbia University. He is the best-selling author of more than 10 books, a former Tibetan Buddhist monk, President of Tibet House in New York City, a close friend of His Holiness the 14th Dalai Lama, and father of five children including the Hollywood actress, Uma. He is a frequent lecturer at venues around the world and in 1997 was chosen by *Time* Magazine as one of the 25 most influential Americans.

When you reach 50, it is an ideal time to think about the meaning of life in a stronger way. To understand the meaning of life, I think you have to confront and deal with the meaning of death.

Life has one kind of meaning if you think of it solely as your physical life, from birth to death. Your consciousness, your sense of being, of subjective presence, is totally identified with your body and brain. When that body and brain are destroyed at death, then you absolutely and forever cease to exist. Living in this context conveys a certain meaning.

But, if what you really are is a soul that goes into future existences in some form or another, then this philosophy of life has another kind of meaning. Particularly if that soul is controlled by a deity and, depending on your belief system, your adherence to a particular religion. In the Buddhist religion, your soul is a product of your own mind and your physical and verbal actions — your evolutionary actions (your karma); it is your own actions that determine what happens to you.

The Buddhist view is that you make yourself, or unmake yourself, all the time. If you behave well and cultivate your good qualities, they will intensify and you'll be better. You'll be happier. You'll be a better person. And if you let yourself go, you'll be worse. That belief becomes the meaning of life — that you do more good things and become a better being.

Think of it as lifting weights. If you lift weights, you get a strong bicep. Nobody awards you with the bicep for lifting the weights. You get it by lifting the weights —

it's the "doing." It changes your arm muscle. Similarly, your moral muscle, your happiness muscle, your wisdom muscle, your intelligence muscle — these things are all changed by what you do with your body and mind.

In my life, I lost an eye at 20. Some people would think that was a terrible, horrible thing. Even I probably felt that way at the time. But it was actually lucky in the long run. Because, even at 20, it gave me a taste of mortality. You normally don't get that opportunity — you dance around, drive too fast, ride your motorcycle, whatever. But it made me realize that life is something you take seriously. What am I doing here? What is the point? What should I try to get out of it?

Your sense of your own mortality can intensify the quest to know what the world is. Just like when you travel somewhere, you want a guidebook. When you know more about it, you get more out of it.

So why wouldn't that apply to life? How could it not be important to know what's really going on? Certainly, we can live just by the myths of others. Many people choose that route: blind faith. We rely on the authority of scientists with their big bang, their double-quad experiment, their quantum quarks. We do whatever we're conditioned to do, without exploring for ourselves. Personally, I'm not satisfied with that. When traveling, don't most of us investigate the best airline, the best hotel, what clothing to bring, what language is spoken? Why not investigate what is the best way to be?

If you haven't explored some of these ideas, 50 is a good time to start. It isn't just about aging. It's what people learn from their years of experience. You're going to have to turn 50 anyway, and there's no way out of it. It's up to you to make it into something worthwhile.

Of course, it is immensely beneficial if you have used your time to develop wisdom and friendliness; if you've realized that the really important things in life are friendships and kindness, that you've been most happy when you've helped others to be happy. Look back and remember the moments of your life that were the great moments — moments when you were caring for another and forgot about yourself.

You can turn the fact that you may not be as limber or as spry as you once were into an advantage. You can be of benefit to others. Because of your age, you now have some authority with the young. You can help them have a good life. Don't spoil them too much, but don't be too hard with them either. Help them find a good path — doing so can make you happy.

If you think, "Hey, what do I get out of being 50?" you're going to be miserable, because it will not be enough. But if you ask, "Well, now I am 50. How can I use that well, to have a better moment?" Then you will find that turning 50 is an enriching experience. Live moment to moment. Help others more. Have more fun with them, and appreciate what is of value.

Regrets can be a great teacher, too. People often find themselves making amends on their deathbed. You've got the opportunity to fix things now, when you reach a milestone like 50, try to anticipate those future regrets and deal with them now.

There are certain truisms that resonate for a reason, one of which comes from the great doctor and author Elisabeth Kübler-Ross. She said she had never met anyone on his or her deathbed who regretted not having spent more time at the office. People do regret not having spent more time with their loved ones. Not having read more poems. Not having looked at more sunsets.

Life is not just survival. People say when they're dying, or when they have a near-death experience, that their life flashes before their eyes. Let that happen now! Even if you live another 50 years, because time is relative and it will seem like a flash before you're there anyway.

As ol' Carlos Castaneda used to say, take death as your adviser and realize how precious moments are, how precious the now is, and live it better. ☼

47

Read the Torah

**You don't have to be Jewish to tackle the Torah.
Turns out Moses has things to say that are relevant
to everyone.**

BY RICHARD SIEGEL

Richard Siegel is the executive director of the National
Foundation for Jewish Culture, an organization dedicated
to strengthening Jewish identity in America through the
arts and humanities. He is the coeditor of *The Jewish Catalog*
(JPS), the insider's guide to the Jewish "counterculture"
of the late 1960s, as well as *The Jewish Almanac* (Bantam
Books) and the Commission Report on the Future of Jewish
Culture in America (NFJC, 2002).

Here are my assumptions:
A. If you are Jewish, you probably had a bar
mitzvah or bat mitzvah when you were 13, but
since then you've rarely been voluntarily inside a synagogue. You know that Jews are called "The People of
the Book," but you've never read the book and don't
really know whether this means one particular book or
books in general.

B. If you are not Jewish, you are curious as to what exactly entitles the Jews to the sobriquet, "People of the Book," particularly given A.

C. If you are approaching 50, or are over 50, you might finally have some time to read books more challenging than summer novels.

So first things first.

There is, in fact, one book, and it is called the Torah. The only problem is that the Torah is a scroll, not a book, and the English translation of it is generally titled *The Five Books of Moses*. So the book we are talking about really contains five books and isn't even a book itself.

In any event, this is THE book that people mean when they talk about the "People of the Book." The reality, however, is that most Jews have never read it in its entirety; a portion of it is read in synagogues each week in sequential order and on an annual cycle. This means that if you had been going to synagogue regularly on Saturday mornings, you would have heard the Torah recited in its entirety at least 37 times since you were 13.

Why isn't it read more? Because this book — the Torah, the Pentateuch, the *The Five Books of Moses* — is intimidating. It bears the weight of being the most studied, poured-over, commented-on book in the history of the world. It is the fundamental text of two of the three Western religions and the jumping off place for the third. How could a nonscholar, a nonprofessional, a noncleric, hope to understand it or its context, its history, its theology?

The reality, however, is that it is pretty straightforward and, for the most part, clearly written. There is no reason not just to pick it up and start reading and finish when you reach the end.

So pick up a copy of the Torah and just start reading. If you can read it in Hebrew, great; if not, don't worry — there are a number of good translations. Here are four contemporary translations, all well-regarded and widely used: *The JPS Bible,* which is the all-time best seller of the Jewish Publication Society of America; *The Schocken Bible,* otherwise known as the Fox Translation, which tries to capture as much of the sound and rhythm of the original Hebrew language as possible; the *Stone Edition,* also known as the Art Scroll Torah, based on the Orthodox perspective and the recently-published *Alter Translation,* written in beautiful style.

Each of these, by the way, also come with commentaries, but for the first read, ignore them. Just start reading. Read a little each day, a couple of chapters, and pretty soon you will have read through it.

Actually, this is not as easy an instruction as it might seem, because you are very likely to be drawn into one thing or another — getting stuck on a word, an idea, a story. Certainly, some of it will probably be familiar to you, if only through osmosis from general society. The Ten Commandments, for instance, or the story of Creation. Some of it, however, will probably be startlingly new, even surprising. There are some pretty odd stories told in there, and even some of the familiar ones have twists that you might not have remembered or learned. So it may be hard to stick to the reading without going off and following one string or another. But keep at it, push through, and keep reading to the end. Write down a list of questions if you want to go back to them later.

Okay, you've read the Torah. Now what? Eat. One of the ways that Judaism reinforces the pleasure of books is by associating reading with food. Children are introduced to the Hebrew Aleph-bet by licking honey off the letters. For adults, when we finish a book, we have a festive meal. So invite some friends and have a dinner party. At some point during the evening, however, you should give a book review. Talk about your most recent read, *The Five Books of Moses*, as you would the new Philip Roth book, the new Tom Clancy novel, or the new movie that you saw, for that matter. What do you think about the characters, plots, structure, language, and messages? It would be even better if everyone in the group had read it, maybe with different translations, because then you could have a good argument. (For any non-Jewish readers, it's important to understand that argumentation is a key element of Jewish life. If something doesn't generate an argument, it pretty much doesn't exist.) But even if you are the only one who has read it, it is very likely that your book review will stimulate an interesting interchange.

What's next? Maybe nothing. Put the book on the shelf, or pass it on to someone else, and enjoy the sense of achievement and satisfaction of having finally read the fundamental text of western civilization. You will be able to strike up cocktail party conversations with a line like, "I was reading the Torah recently, and found something interesting . . . ."

If, on the other hand, your interest is piqued, there is a world of follow-ups. Buy the other three translations. Then pick one and start reading from the beginning all over again. Only this time, when you get to a passage that raises a question, look up how the others translate it. You have now entered into the "Sea of Torah" — you're not just reading, you're studying. Enjoy the process, and remember to have a meal each time you finish the book.

48

Time to start unlearning

Fifty is a great time to forget everything you ever thought you knew about God — and start over.

BY FATHER JOSEPH KELLY, S.J.

Father Joseph Kelly, S.J., the youngest of seven children, was born in County Offaly, Ireland. He joined the Jesuits in 1949 and after 14 years of study, was ordained. He took his undergraduate degree in English language and literature in 1954 at University College, Dublin. He came to the United States in 1965 for postgraduate studies at Cornell and Loyola. He served as chaplain at St. Peter's College in New Jersey for 20 years. In 1993, he joined St. Malachy's, The Actors Chapel in New York City as parochial vicar. Father Kelly passed away in December 2008, just as he was about to return to work at St. Peter's College.

Russell Baker once wrote a whimsical article about founding a "University of Unlearning." In it, he wrote, the more "facts" one was able to jettison the better. The degree would be a "Non-Bachelor of Un-Arts" and would be given to those who clearly manifested their ignorance of factual knowledge. Being a priest, this naturally made me think of the Catholic Church.

I looked at the word "unlearn." I thought to myself, that's something I need to do. Gradually I began to go back over much of what I was taught as a "practicing Catholic" and started the painful, but fruitful, process of "unlearning." I took a good look at all I had been taught about God, sin, hell, sex, purgatory and, most of all, what I hadn't been taught about love. I suddenly had the novel idea to use my God-given intelligence and its attendant right to question, believing that God's benign and loving spirit would guide me as I tried to free myself from some of the lopsided legacies and false images that were passed off to me as "religion" or, worse still, "the will of God."

So much of what has been instilled in me, in all Catholics, is solely church-imposed, mere human dogma, always bristling with eternal sanctions of hellfire. There was so little talk of love, so much more talk of rules and regulations. Since I've passed 50, I look over my amassed "knowledge" and find that "unlearning" much of this material, to get at the underlying principles, to get to the heart of the matter, is the clearest path to God. A Jesuit spiritual author once wrote, "The longest journey in the spiritual life is from the head to the heart." "Unlearning" is an important step on that journey.

Of course, even the beginning of this journey is immediately problematic. You see, I was born with original sin on my soul. That gets me off to a pretty poor start. If I died without ever being baptized, then my fate, and that of all poor pagan babies for that matter, is eternally sealed — hellfire forever. I was born with what the Irish catechism called a "propensity to evil." Nobody ever mentioned that I might have a "propensity to good." In 43 years as a Jesuit priest, I have performed many baptisms. As I look into the innocent eyes of a baby, is it my church or my God that compels me to think, "Come here you little bundle of 'propensity to evil' and God will straighten out your immortal soul"? Clearly, a bit of "unlearning" might be beneficial.

Let's have a look at the obligation to go to Mass on Sunday. Rather a mixed message. On the one hand God affirms his unconditional love for us. On the other He tells us, "You've got to come and see me once a week, as well as on the special Holy Days of Obligation. If you don't come, and you don't have a good reason why not, then that's a mortal sin, and you know that means hellfire for all eternity again." How does one RSVP to that sort of invitation? Would a friend or lover's issuing of that kind of ultimatum be indicative of a healthy relationship? Looks like more "unlearning" might help here, too.

In a book I once read and enjoyed, *Good Goats: Healing Our Image Of God,* the authors address God's image problem by asking, "Do you see God as your prosecuting attorney or your defense attorney?" Our answer to that question tells us a lot about how we see God — and love. Is my God one who truly loves me and will stand up for me, or one who is only bent on judging me, twice no less, at the Particular Judgement and the General Judgement. The question then becomes, do we have some serious "unlearning" to do about God?

Many are angry at a church that has left them confused and bewildered. Ecclesiastical power was abused, scandals surfaced. And the tragedy now is that for many Catholics the church, which could be such a source of spiritual support, is seen as largely irrelevant. The voices of those who do have words of hope and love are not listened to. Because, too often we set out to make people feel guilty, and we are now reaping the fruit of what we sowed.

So, finally we must ask how one goes about the "unlearning" process. I think it will involve loving and that might mean risk and disruption. By the time we are 50, perhaps we are wise enough to try to see our God in a new light. Going to Sunday Mass should be something we *want* to do. The Sacrament of Confession should be an encounter with a loving and compassionate God who knows our weaknesses long before we try to express them. Our faith should be something God has given us to make us free, not constrain us. The ultimate goal is to love and be loved. This sounds so trite, so easy to say, so hard to do, but I think the person who loves and is loved will still always be "unlearning," because such a one is open and resilient.

In his wonderful book *The Four Loves*, C.S. Lewis writes about the dangers of closing one's heart:

> "To love at all is to be vulnerable. Love anything, and your heart will certainly be wrung and possibly be broken. If you want to make sure of keeping it intact, you must give your heart to no one, not even to an animal. Wrap it carefully round with hobbies and little luxuries; avoid all entanglements; lock it up safe in the casket or coffin of your selfishness. But in that casket — safe, dark, motionless, airless — it will change. It will not be broken; it will become unbreakable, impenetrable, irredeemable. The alternative to tragedy, or at least to the risk of tragedy, is damnation. The only place outside Heaven you can be perfectly safe from all the dangers and perturbations of love is Hell."

God wants us to be more than we are, or more than we think we can be. This means a commitment to the possibly painful but ultimately freeing and most important, loving process of "unlearning." What better time than your 50s to matriculate from Russell Baker's University! ☀

49

Live your faith and enjoy the world

Islamic tradition says we should live as if we're going to live forever, and die tomorrow. A Muslim cleric weighs in on how to strike this tricky balance.

BY FAROQUE KHAN, M.D.

Faroque Khan, M.D., is the spokesman and president of the Islamic Center of Long Island, he is a Master at the American College of Physicians, and is the author of three books including *Story of a Mosque in America*. He has served as advisor on the television program *Our Muslim Neighbor* with God Squad hosts Rabbi Marc Gellman and Msgr. Tom Hartman. Khan is the recipient of numerous awards, among them, the American College of Physicians Laureate Award, the American Federation of Muslims from India's Excellence Award, and *Newsday's* 2004 Everyday Hero Award.

For Muslims, it is the 40th year that holds special significance, so by 50 you will have had 10 more years to reflect.

Muslims believe that we are in this world for a short period of time and the real life, the eternal life, is the hereafter. Everyone will die, then there will be a resurrection, a Day of Accountability. And on that day, God decides whether one goes to Heaven or Hell.

A Muslim's goal is to aim for the Heaven. How does one do that? The guidance is in the Quran (Koran), which is the Scripture we believe in. We believe in the Old Testament, the New Testament, and that the Quran is the final Testament.

Our faith instructs us that you have to do for your neighbors what you would do for yourself. Now, the neighbor is not just the guy down the street; the neighbor is also the man in Indonesia/Somalia/Palestine who has no home right now. These are the issues that will be examined by God on the Day of Judgment. God says, "I left you in this world. I gave you good health. I gave you resources. What did you do with them? Did you follow the instructions? Or did you behave as though this world is the only life; there's nothing else to look forward to?"

Those instructions are sharing, caring — the Ten Commandments basically. Our "instructions" in the Quran are an extension and refinement of the Judeo-Christian tenets, a follow-up on them, if you will. There are some differences with Christian beliefs: For instance, we believe that Jesus was a great prophet (peace be upon him), but not that he was the physical form of God — beyond that Muslim beliefs are really much the same as those of Christians. Do for your neighbor what you would do for yourself. Love thy neighbor.

Islamic tradition holds that a human being is a very special creature endowed with intellect, choice, and free will. At the same time, there is an awareness that we are dependent upon a higher power. Basically our earthly life is a test. If we pass that test, we are promised eternal bliss. But there is a misconception about what constitutes that bliss. The hereafter is not like our earthly life. It is not sensual. The Quran says that women and men who do good will be given companionship that is pure, be surrounded by 70 virgins (beings of purity). Some people have misconstrued "purity" to mean virginity.

But years of experience as you grow and mature bring you to new levels of understanding. As a physician, sometimes I have wondered whether the Scriptures are real. But after my extensive study, I believe there's no question that the information in the Quran has come from a "higher" source. Passage after passage in the Quran deals with space exploration, oceans and underwater life, fertilization followed by stages of embryo and fetus development including explanations detailing when the embryo/fetus develops senses such as sight and hearing and so on. As a physician, I know that 1,450 years ago, the technology didn't exist from which to draw that information.

The words of the Quran and all of its teachings we believe to be the word of God transmitted directly from Him through the Angel Gabriel to prophet Mohammad (*pbuh*), over a period of 23 years. As prophet Mohammed (*pbuh*) received these revelations, because he was unable to read and write, he spoke them aloud, and they were carefully transcribed by his companions. He thought he was going mad. But even though he didn't understand what he was hearing, scholars in his community assured him that he was prophesying the word of God. So, for Muslims, the Quran is a great miracle and to this day, no one has been able to challenge its authenticity. All the instructions are in there.

In the Quran, God assures us that everyone makes mistakes, even the prophets. At some point, there comes a time when you examine your actions and think, "I wish I hadn't done that," or "I wish I had behaved differently." So ask for forgiveness. God is very merciful. At the same time, this doesn't justify making the same mistake over and over again and asking for forgiveness for the same sins. For every action, there is a consequence.

The classic example is the story of Adam and Eve. We are

taught that they were in Heaven and they had free reign. And God said, "Do everything except don't go near the apple tree." They both disobeyed, they both were punished. And the punishment was to leave Heaven, go to Earth. And here we are, the descendents of Adam and Eve. They asked for forgiveness, they were forgiven, but there were consequences.

So understand that if you make a mistake, forgiveness doesn't necessarily mitigate the consequences. But the 114 chapters in the Quran start with: "In the name of God, the most gracious and most merciful." In the Islamic context, the concept of God and His mercy takes precedence over God and His punishment.

And remember: It is not for us to judge who is doing good, and who is not doing good. That is clearly outlined in the Quran. Don't pass judgment on others: to you, your way; to me, my way. Proselytizing is not permitted.

Islamic tradition says: Live as if you're going to live forever. And live as if you're going to die tomorrow. You've got to have both. *Deen* and *dunya*. *Deen* means faith. *Dunya* means world.

Live your faith and enjoy the world. In Islamic tradition, it is only with God's permission that we will die. You cannot predict the time for that. So be prepared.

It can happen on the most unexpected day. In your 50s, you may be nowhere near your deathbed, but we are so often called to the mosque for those who have died unexpectedly.

As you move along, hopefully you mature. You learn more, you understand more. You become more introspective and less materialistic. You become more spiritual and do what you're expected to do in a more focused manner.

50

Trade strength for wisdom

Being the toughest person in the room is good.
Being the most compassionate is better.

BY HAROLD S. KUSHNER

Harold Kushner is Rabbi Laureate of Temple Israel, Natick, Massachusetts, and the author of eight best-selling books, most notably *When Bad Things Happen to Good People.*

What is the wisdom we gain as we turn 50, wisdom that we may have lacked when we were younger? For men, we can stop seeing other men as rivals and come to see them as colleagues, perhaps even as students. At around age 50, we should begin to feel the need to mentor, to pass on what we have learned to a younger generation, lest all that experience vanish with us when our lives end. The fires of competitiveness have banked and we find it easier to relate to other men.

There is something profoundly gratifying, surprisingly so, about no longer seeing other men as rivals and obstacles to our success. Men in their 50s will find it easier to have male friends, not just buddies to fish with or watch a ballgame with, but real friends to share their innermost thoughts with, the way women have friends. An acquaintance of mine, a minister to a small church in a working-class suburb, confessed to me one day that when he turned 50, he realized to his embarrassment that he had spent the last 20 years hoping for one of his friends or colleagues to fall ill or be caught up in a scandal, so that he could apply to their more affluent church. Now he was prepared to give up that unworthy dream and become a mentor to younger ministers in the area. The thirst for success had given way to a concern for the lasting impact that he would have on the generation after him. I suspect it is not a coincidence that, when I was in my late 40s, I began to give fewer sermons and write books instead, and took on an assistant rabbi to whom I could be a mentor.

For a woman turning 50, the challenge is in a sense an opposite one, to move beyond living for and through others and focus more on oneself. If you have spent the first five decades of your life graduating from being someone's daughter to being someone's girlfriend to being someone's wife to being someone's mother and then grandmother, this can be a joyous time of discovery — a time in your life to figure out what it would mean to be someone in your own right. You are not being selfish or irresponsible; you are reaching for wholeness.

The psychoanalyst Carl Jung suggested that every human infant has the potential for masculine and feminine dimensions to his or her personality. When society teaches little boys to be tough and ambitious and teaches little girls to be sensitive and live through others, it compels us to neglect half of our human potential. Midlife, life after 50, is a time to go back and fill in the spaces we might have left blank when we were growing up.

My traditions teach me that wisdom is of greater value than physical strength, and that therefore we should rejoice when we reach that stage in our lives when physical agility begins to decline but wisdom increases.

The wisdom of middle age should include expanding your social network, making new friends to replace friends lost to distance or illness. It should include finding new interests, especially ones that stretch your mind. It should include a sense of obligation to give back to your community and your world some of what life has blessed you with. But most of all, it should include a sense of optimism, the feeling that, in the words of Robert Browning, "The best is yet to be, the last of life for which the first was made."

About the Editors

Allison Kyle Leopold, COMMISSIONING EDITOR, is an award-winning editor and journalist, the owner and editor-in-chief of AKL Studio, a magazine and book development company, and editor of special interest publications for *Country Living Magazine.* She has authored more than a dozen books. Leopold began her career with *Seventeen Magazine* before joining *Harper's Bazaar* and *Vogue* magazines. She was editor of numerous special interest lifestyle publications for *Woman's Day,* travel editor of *Child* magazine, editor-in-chief of *Flair* magazine, and editor-in-chief of a regional magazine group.

Gerit Quealy, COMMISSIONING EDITOR, is a journalist, author, and editor in New York City with extensive experience in the entertainment, travel, wellness, and lifestyle areas. The coauthor of two books, *Fashion: Careers Without College* with Kathleen Beckett and *Wedding Flowers* with Allison Kyle Leopold, Quealy is also the author of a humor book entitled *Are You My Husband?* As deputy editor of AKL Studio Editorial, she has worked on projects for clients ranging from the Metropolitan Museum of Art to Avon, in addition to serving as senior editor at *Flair* magazine. She also writes regularly for *The New York Times.*

Debra Gordon, COMMISSIONING EDITOR, is an award-winning journalist who has been writing about health and healthcare for more than 15 years. She began her career as a reporter at the *Virginian Pilot* newspaper in Norfolk,

Virginia, then became the medical reporter at the *Orange County Register* in Southern California. She has been a full-time freelance health and medical writer and editor since 2000 and has authored or coauthored numerous consumer health books. Her work has also appeared in *Health, Family Circle, Better Homes & Gardens, Good Housekeeping, Reader's Digest,* and *Diabetes Today* magazines.

Brian O'Connell, COMMISSIONING EDITOR, is a Pennsylvania-based freelance writer and editor with 12 years of experience covering political and business news and trends. A former Wall Street bond trader, he has contributed to dozens of national publications, including *The Chicago Tribune, The Wall Street Journal, Newsweek, Philadelphia Magazine, USA Weekend, Men's Health, Entrepreneur Magazine,* and *CBS News Market Watch.* He has authored 10 books, including two best-selling Book of the Month Club selections. In addition, O'Connell has appeared as an expert commentator on business and finance issues on CNN, *International NewsFirst,* Web TV, and *Fox News.*

Sarah Mahoney, SERIES EDITOR, is a contributing editor for *More, Parents,* and *Prevention.* Her work has appeared in *Woman's Day, Better Homes & Gardens, Reader's Digest,* and *The New York Times.* Now based in rural Maine, she formerly held several top-level editing positions at women's magazines, including editor of *Ladies' Home Journal,* editor-in-chief of *Fitness* magazine, and executive editor of *Parents* magazine. She started her career as a reporter at *Advertising Age* before joining United Press International as a business writer. She has made frequent television appearances on, among others, *Good Morning America, The Early Show,* CNN, CBS, Court TV, Fox, *Entertainment Tonight,* and Lifetime.

Acknowledgments

For their help and support with this project, I would like to thank Madeleine Beckman, Janet Cole, Vickie Peslak Hyman, Michelle Keith, Dena Moss, Marie-Claire Sillick, Jody Shields, and Robin Stern.

Allison Kyle Leopold

This book would not have been possible without the help of the following people: Christopher Durang, Francis Guinan, Jennifer Swihart, Gilda Squire, Charles Salzberg, Giulia Melucci, Michael Gooch-Breault, Brian Shaffer, Jensine Andresen, Melissa May, Steven May, Don Codling, Mark K. Anderson, Sherry Anderson, Joanna Parson, Dee Pelletier, Tom Kelly, Wendy Zoller, and Rahadyan Sastrowardoyo.

Gerit Quealy

I'd like to acknowledge the authors of the essays, who willingly submitted to several rounds of edits without complaining and who volunteered so much of their time and effort.

Debra Gordon

I'd like to thank the essayists who contributed their time and efforts to this book. Each is at the top of his or her profession and each brought a considerable amount of cachet to the book. Special thanks also go to Elisabeth Flynn and Gretchen Cassidy, who proved invaluable in helping edit and organize the financial services and career management sections of the book.

Brian O'Connell

Credits: continued from copyright page

Stop complaining © 2005 Garrison Keillor; *Look for what's hopeful and go with it* © 2005 Wendy Wasserstein; *Write your own top ten list* © 2005 Patricia Farrell, Ph.D.; *Find your inner elegy* © 2005 Billy Collins; *Keep a sense of adventure* © 2005 Marianne Williamson; *Stop obsessing about your flaws* © 2005 Bobbi Brown; *Put your best face forward* © 2005 Valerie J. Ablaza, M.D.; *Wear comfortable clothes* © 2005 Diane von Furstenberg; *Take your self back* © 2005 Erica Jong; *Take a hike* © 2005 Kristina Hurrell; *Limber up. Get flex-y with it* © 2005 Jonathan Fields; *Indulge yourself in a playground fantasy* © 2005 Luis Santeiro; *Learn to belly dance* © 2005 TaRessa Stovall; *Power up your tennis game* © 2005 Angela Buxton; *Sit still: meditation is medicinal* © 2005 Robert H. Schneider, M.D.; *Eat like a caveman* © 2005 Fred Pescatore, M.D.; *Take heart* © 2005 David Katz, M.D.; *Bone up* © 2005 Michael R. Wilson, M.D.; *Buff up your brain* © 2005 Bill Beckwith, Ph.D.; *Stop squinting* © 2005 Brian S. Boxer Wachler, M.D.; *Stop the flash: eat soy and flax* © 2005 Dorothy Foltz-Gray; *Look within: get a colonoscopy* © 2005 Patricia L. Raymond, M.D.; *Reappraise yourself* © 2005 Mary Furlong; *Stay curious, be relevant, and THRIVE!* © 2005 David Ebony; *Hire yourself* © 2005 Alan Weiss; *Stop proving yourself* © 2005 Susan Seidelman; *Now that you're tops at what you do, teach* © 2005 Eleanor D'Antuono; *Pay off your mortgage* © 2005 Suze Orman; *Bulk up your portfolio's defense* © 2005 Bill Gross; *Rethink your insurance strategy* © 2005 Richard Bowren; *Strengthen your will* © 2005 Rebecca Smolen; *Budget to your 100th birthday* © 2007 Eric Friedman; *Get smart about the IRS* © 2007 Bradford Hall, CPA; *Embrace your inner Trump* © 2005 Jo-Anne Atwell; *Give something back* © 2005 Lorna Wendt; *Get your mojo working* © 2005 Marc C. Gittelman, M.D.; *Drive a race car* © 2005 Ed McCabe; *Play golf in Scotland* © 2005 Bill Daniels; *Throw a slow-dance party* © 2005 Nelson George; *Lose the list* © 2005 Peter Greenberg; *Go fishing* © 2005 James Prosek; *Check your "turning 50" horoscope* © 2005 Kat Lane; *Jump off a bridge* © 2005 Mark Fenton; *Never cease the mental fight* © 2005 Harold Bloom; *Don't go off the deep end* © 2005 Gary Jobson; *Let your life flash before your eyes* © 2005 Robert Thurman, Ph.D.; *Read the Torah* © 2005 Richard Siegel; *Time to start unlearning* © 2005 Father Joseph Kelly, S.J.; *Live your faith and enjoy the world* © 2005 Faroque Khan, M.D.; *Trade strength for wisdom* © 2005 Harold S. Kushner